"So unique is their life, if only one percent of our citizenry would live with the imagination and intentionality that Mark and Lisa Scandrette do, the world would be a demonstrably better place. With *Belonging and Becoming*, the Scandrettes build on the bedrock of their twenty-five year marriage and their winsome, faithful work of caring for people and place. We cannot endorse this couple too highly. They represent a way of being and doing that exceeds admirable, landing at 'Wow!'"

Andi Ashworth and Charlie Peacock, writer and record producer, cofounders of Art House America

"So happy this book was written, so mad it wasn't written thirty years ago! I know that Mark and Lisa did not just write this book, but they have also lived it. And in the living of it, they make room for various expressions of the values-based, thoughtful approach to parenting that we all aspire to. Our world, our neighborhoods, and our souls will be the richer for the reading and practice of these pages."

Nancy Ortberg, author of *Looking for God*

"Mark and Lisa Scandrette offer tangible hope for families by both their example and their wise instruction in *Belonging and Becoming*. They articulate ways families can live toward God's justice and goodness in the world as well as support one another in mutual thriving. They embrace the internal and external call of each family to love one another and be a blessing to the entire neighborhood. As a parent and practitioner, I appreciate the rich vocabulary they've given us with this book!"

Kelley Nikondeha, Communities of Hope, Burundi

"For the past two decades, Mark and Lisa Scandrette have been at the leading edge of creative faith practices and community engagement, all while nurturing a family life that models the way of Jesus. At last they have put these passions together in a book that's sure to be a go-to resource for families of all kinds seeking to grow one another up into wise, engaged, and faith-filled disciples. By sharing their best family practices and providing tools to help readers create their own, the Scandrettes have created a resource that's sure to evoke deep refection and thoughtful practices for a family life of faith."

David M. Csinos, Atlantic School of Theology, executive director, Faith Forward

"Mark and Lisa Scandrette understand that thriving families are born of gracious intentionality. I know as you read these pages you'll find both intention and grace: practical wisdom and insights along with the encouragement to live with forgiveness, empathy, compassion, and a will to keep trying."
Nate Ernsberger, speakers' director, Compassion International

"Mark and Lisa's vision for family life is both challenging and inspiring, and Aaron and I are so thankful to have learned from their example over the years of our friendship. This book is a gift: intelligent and brave, prophetic and grounded. I recommend it for any parent who wants to be wiser, more soulful, and more imaginative in their parenting—which is all of us, right?"
Shauna Niequist, author of *Bread & Wine* and *Present Over Perfect*

Belonging
and
Becoming

CREATING A THRIVING
FAMILY CULTURE

MARK & LISA
SCANDRETTE

WITH CONTRIBUTIONS BY HAILEY JOY SCANDRETTE

IVP Books

An imprint of InterVarsity Press
Downers Grove, Illinois

InterVarsity Press
P.O. Box 1400, Downers Grove, IL 60515-1426
ivpress.com
email@ivpress.com

InterVarsity Press® is the book-publishing division of InterVarsity Christian Fellowship/USA®, a
movement of students and faculty active on campus at hundreds of universities, colleges and schools
of nursing in the United States of America, and a member movement of the International Fellowship
of Evangelical Students. For information about local and regional activities, visit intervarsity.org.

All Scripture quotations, unless otherwise indicated, are taken from THE HOLY BIBLE,
NEW INTERNATIONAL VERSION®, NIV® Copyright © 1973, 1978, 1984, 2011 by Biblica,
Inc.™ Used by permission. All rights reserved worldwide.

While any stories in this book are true, some names and identifying information may have been
changed to protect the privacy of individuals.

Cover design: Cindy Kiple
Interior design: Jeanna Wiggins
Images: Graphic tree illustration: ©galbiati/iStockphoto
Graphic icons: © appleuzr/iStockphoto

ISBN 978-0-8308-4489-0 (print)
ISBN 978-0-8308-9216-7 (digital)

Printed in the United States of America ∞

Library of Congress Cataloging-in-Publication Data
A catalog record for this book is available from the Library of Congress.

P 25 24 23 22 21 20 19 18 17 16 15 14 13 12 11 10 9 8 7 6 5 4 3 2 1

Y 34 33 32 31 30 29 28 27 26 25 24 23 22 21 20 19 18 17 16

To Hailey,
your bright light calls us to justice

To Noah,
your gentle strength invites us to know and explore

To Isaiah,
your sparkle and warmth bring laughter and peace

This book comes from our shared story of belonging and becoming, and the best is yet to come.

Contents

1

A Thriving Family Lives from a Vision

AMANDA AND LUKE ARE PARENTS to three children under three, including a set of twins. "Managing our daily schedule is so hectic, it's like we live in a giant hamster wheel," Amanda says. The day starts with a bang when the twins wake up at five thirty, then everyone needs to get fed and dressed so that Luke can walk their older son to preschool while Amanda hands the twins off to a caregiver before rushing to catch the train to work. "Our schedule is so complicated," Luke says. "If one thing doesn't go *just* right—if the babysitter is running late or one of the kids gets sick—it throws the whole day off, and we're left scrambling just to keep up."

Carlos confides, "You know something is wrong when I wake up in the morning and reach for my smartphone before kissing my wife good morning—or I'm at the breakfast table looking down at my phone instead of talking to the kids while they munch their cereal. I really want to be a connected father and husband, but it's so easy to be distracted."

"Before I had children," Maria says, "I thought of myself as someone who really lives out their values. I had time to be involved in my community, meeting the needs of neighbors and supporting causes I care about. Now my greatest achievement seems to be a full night's sleep and getting everyone where they need to be on time. I fear I've given up my dreams and ideals. I'm doing what seems urgent, but maybe not what's important."

Perhaps you can relate to the sentiments of these parents. Many of us live lives of distraction, hurry, worry or striving. We desire the wholeness of close relationships, soulful work and rooted vitality, but the everyday demands of life, our expectations and those of our society often leave us feeling fragmented. We have high aspirations for how we want to connect with our children and spouses and for what we hope to provide, but we struggle to find the time, energy and support to fulfill many competing desires and needs. No wonder so many of us feel stretched and tired.

How can a family thrive?

When the two of us met, we almost immediately recognized what we had in common: a passion for families and a desire to create a thriving family of our own. We spent the first five years of our marriage working with underresourced families through a faith-based nonprofit, setting up kids' clubs in low-income neighborhoods and government housing projects. We had the privilege of being invited into the lives of many families and witnessed both their beauty and their pain.

Though we didn't yet have children of our own, our apartment became a place of refuge for the children of parents grappling with addiction, mental illness, sexual trauma and the lingering effects of displacement and war. Kids would wander over to our apartment on nights when Mom or Dad were drinking. We hosted family meals with nutritious food, table conversations and games—trying our best to supplement the warmth, nurture and safety their families struggled to provide.

Perhaps naively, we believed that our time and affection could mitigate the lack of thriving experienced in many of their families. But as these children reached adolescence, the latent effects began to manifest. As teenagers, many of the kids we cared for became parents themselves or ended up in juvenile detention. Several died too early through violence.

Our work with children and parents sensitized us to the dynamics present in healthy families that are often absent in families that fail to thrive. On wooded paths along Minnesota lakes, we went for long walks and talked about the kind of family we hoped to create together. We imagined a household of laughter, fun and deep connections. We wanted an awareness of divine purpose and presence to permeate our lives and shape our decisions. We envisioned doing meaningful work together, using our gifts to serve. We hoped to open our lives to others, especially to those who struggle and suffer. And we desired to live gratefully, creatively and sustainably.

Envisioning the kind of family we wanted to be was a start, but it would take a lifetime to enact. In the early years of our marriage, we thought we were getting traction on the life we'd imagined, but as our three children, Hailey, Noah and Isaiah, came along—one after the other over three years—life became more complicated. We didn't get an uninterrupted night of sleep for five years. That time was a blur of diaper changes, feedings, teething, earaches and laundry.

Before kids, we felt supremely confident about our skills for re-lating; we'd even done our university studies in family counseling and early childhood education. But living out those skills day to day proved to be much harder. With kids, we felt more pressure about money and career, and the competing demands of work and home revealed our unhealthy patterns for dealing with stress. We became conscious of the gap between the family we wanted to be and the family we actually were. With so many more decisions to make together, it was some-times difficult to come to an agreement. It began to feel like our hopes, dreams and ideals for family life were slipping away.

Conventional wisdom told us that we should put our deepest dreams on hold in order to provide our kids with the American dream:

a safe neighborhood, good schools and upward mobility. Just before our son Noah was born, we bought our first house. Mark took a job as minister to families at a local church and started graduate school. During those years, Lisa stayed home to care for our children while Mark commuted to work each day. We had a home in the country, a minivan in the garage and a busy schedule of activities. Life for our growing family was good and stable, but it felt fragmented. We were succeeding in one or two areas but found it challenging to make all the parts of life work together. We'd always imagined our family being at the center of a life of shared service and adventure, not segmented like it was.

One of the best things we did at that time was *stop and reflect*. Had we settled for less? Did we like where we were going? Was normal working? What were we teaching our kids by our choices? The ache of these questions put us on a search for a more integrated path for family life.

We took the time to *explore new possibilities*. We considered what we appreciated about our families of origin. Lisa grew up on a farm, the youngest of six children, and her parents provided foster care to more than one hundred children over the years, eventually adding three more brothers to the family through adoption. We admired their family culture of care and hospitality. Mark grew up in the city with three sisters, in a military family that was very close. We appreciated their family culture of honesty, clear communication and intentionality.

We also read books about creating healthy family culture, and we paid careful attention to the habits and rhythms of families we knew that seemed to be thriving:

- "I like the gentle but direct way Debbie talks to her son."

- "I think it's cool that the Carlsgaards get together in the late evening with their teenagers to catch up, pray and hang out."

- "I like the way Lynette and Ger take their kids on weekly one-on-one dates."

Inspired by what we saw, read and experienced, we resolved to *take new life-giving steps* toward creating a thriving family culture.

We've spent the past twenty-five years chasing after the whole and integrated life we were created for as a family. Through this book, we hope to share the joys, failures and successes of that journey and to introduce you to other parents and families seeking to create thriving family cultures. Our daughter, Hailey, who is now twenty-two, will also offer a reflection on her family experience at the end of each chapter.

THE BIBLE AND FAMILIES

If you're familiar with the phrase "the biblical family," you may get the impression that the Bible presents a romantic or idealized view of family life. But by comparison, the families portrayed in Scripture would probably make your family look like the cheery family of a 1970s sitcom. In the earliest family story, Cain murders his brother, Abel. Abraham the patriarch tries to pass off his wife as his sister, and this habit of deception transfers from one generation to the next. Tamar, the daughter of King David, is raped by her brother; David's son, Absalom, marshals an army against his father. Polygamy was common, and women were often treated like property. Even Jesus had family problems. At one point his mother and brothers thought he was crazy and tried to take charge of him. When we feel the struggle and challenge of family life, we're in good company.

The Bible is realistic about the pain but also hopeful about the possibilities for family life. The prophet Malachi predicted that the work of the Messiah would "turn the hearts of [parents] to their children, and the hearts of the children to their [parents]." The revelation of Jesus opened up new horizons for what it means to be human and, consequently, new possibilities for families. Jesus described this as the reality of the kingdom of God, or a life of shalom, wholeness or harmony under God's care. It's the kind of life we were created for, in which we find our truest identity as God's beloved children, learn to work as agents of healing, act from a sense of abundance and trust, relate to one another from a greater source of love, and experience peace and power in the midst of the stresses and struggles of life.

Whatever your family experience has been, it's not the end of the story. Families can grow and change, and we have a lifetime to seek healing and embrace wholeness in our family relationships. Derek, a fifty-five-year-old father with three adult sons, was raised by a cold, strict and demanding father. "But whenever I see my dad now," Derek says, "he hugs and kisses me and tells me he loves me. I can't believe it's the same man!" Growing up, Rosella's father was so abusive that she and her siblings were removed from the home and placed in foster care. Eventually her dad got into recovery. Now she's in her thirties, raising kids of her own, and they have reconnected. Rosella says, "My father has become one of my greatest allies and a source of spiritual support. He's becoming the father I never had."

We noticed this same phenomenon while listening to stories from our own families. When Mark was studying family systems in graduate school, he interviewed his grandmother for an assignment. She told him, "I was amazed by how deliberate and calm your father was when he spoke to you when you were small—even when he was disciplining you. I thought, *Where did my son learn to communicate like that? It definitely wasn't from his father and me!*"

As we open our lives to God's light and love, we can expect newness to come to our family relationships. God has a way of life for us that works, that connects us to divine presence, to ourselves and to one another. And it awakens us to the wonder, aches and needs of our world. Jesus had this to say to weary families like ours:

Are you tired? Worn out?... Come to me. Get away with me and you'll recover your life. I'll show you how to take a real rest. Walk with me and work with me—watch how I do it. Learn the unforced rhythms of grace. I won't lay anything heavy or ill-fitting on you. Keep company with me and you'll learn to live freely and lightly.

This invitation to wholeness and vitality is very good news for families. If our inherited ways of thinking, behaving and relating are wearing us out and making our lives fragmented, Jesus offers a radical, integral alternative. What would our lives look like if we let them be shaped more by this vision than by the values and priorities of a hurried and fragmented culture?

In our culture we encounter all kinds of competing expectations about what it means to be successful as parents. St. Paul suggested that a parent's true job is to "take [their children] by the hand and lead them in the way of the Master." That's a refreshing view of success: helping each other live in the freedom and lightness that Jesus modeled and taught. Perhaps the highest aspiration a family can have is to help one another discover the whole and integrated lives we were created for.

MADE FOR A LIFE OF FLOURISHING

When our kids were small, our refrigerator was constantly decorated with crayon drawings they proudly presented to us. Amid the pictures of butterflies, monsters, fire trucks and princesses, there would inevitably be a stick figure drawing of our family holding hands, lined up from shortest to tallest, usually in front of our house, with a bright yellow sun and birds flapping their wings in the sky above. The pictures were often narrated: "Mommy, that's you and Papa, and me and Noah and Isaiah." Like many children, our kids drew and told stories to name and understand their world. Sometimes we'd ask a question about the drawing to take the conversation further. "What do you like about our family?" or "How do we care for each other?" or "What is a family for?"

How would you answer the question "What is a family for?" For the purpose of this book, we'd like to offer this vision of a thriving family culture: *A thriving family is a place of belonging and becoming, where each person feels safe, cared for and loved, and is supported to develop who they are for the good of the world.*

Families come in all shapes and sizes. Some families have two parents, others have one, and still others have three or more. There are families with and without children, and children come into families by birth, by adoption and sometimes simply through love. Whatever the makeup of your household, we believe your family can be a space of belonging, where each person feels safe, loved, cherished and cared for, and a place of becoming, where you help one another discover and develop how you participate in the greater good God desires.

Too much talk about the importance of family can make some of us roll our eyes and sigh. Loyalty to family and tribe can sometimes mask a fearful and myopic focus on "me and mine." We see this dramatically portrayed by the television antihero who justifies acts of violence and greed as efforts to provide for and protect their family. A "family first" philosophy has been used over millennia to rationalize aggression against immigrants, neighboring villages and nations.

Family can easily become an idol. Jesus knew this and often pushed his listeners to think beyond the boundaries of their biological families and tribal allegiances. We're invited to love and care for our immediate families, while also appreciating that we're part of the larger human family. The trajectory of a thriving family is outward toward an ever-expanding embrace of the shalom that God desires for all people and all of creation. We seek to care for, connect and belong to one another so we can be prepared to seek the greater good of all—so that all families on earth can thrive.

So much of our formation as people happens and is lived out in the context of family. That's where we develop our identity, where we learn what to value and how to relate to others and navigate the challenges and stresses of life. Family is an important context of formation, not only for children, but for parents as well. We are all in the process of becoming who we were made to be for the good of the world. This is why we hope you keep in mind that this is not a book about parenting but a book about creating a thriving family culture. It's about how your family can relate as a living system that encourages and supports belonging and becoming for all its members through every age and stage of life. You can seek to create a culture together—a way of life with common beliefs, values, practices and symbols—that supports thriving.

For many of us, the word *family* stirs up a complex mix of emotions. You might think of cherished memories from your childhood or of the abuse, betrayal or neglect you experienced through the people you trusted to care for you. Those of us who are parents may think of precious times of closeness with a child or sadness and regret over mistakes we've made. All of these reactions point to the power family has to impact our lives in both positive and negative ways.

Over the years, we've had the privilege of walking with many friends who had very difficult family-of-origin experiences and who have searched for guidance about how to parent differently than they were parented. What surprises us is the number of people we know who were raised in stable and religiously devout homes who have said, "We feel like we know more about what we don't want to be as a family than what we do want to be."

What accounts for this strong reaction? Further conversation often reveals the gap many people feel between what their parents said they believed or valued and how things actually played out in the life of their family. As one young man put it, "We went to church and thought of ourselves as good Christians, but what really drove our family culture was partisan politics and the pursuit of personal wealth." Religious belief by itself doesn't bring about the healing and wholeness we desire in our families. To experience true healing and transformation, life-giving ways must be integrated into the details of daily life.

Another factor may be that our society has changed so much since the days when many of us were being parented twenty, thirty or forty years ago. Technology, the economy and many of our social institutions have shifted dramatically. With the rising costs of education, housing and health care, families face new economic challenges. Our sensibilities about life and our consciousness about the world are also evolving. We live in a much more connected, complex and diverse world than the one most of us were born into. This landscape requires new skills and approaches to parenting and family life.

How can we create a home that honors the best of where we come from and embraces the emerging challenges and opportunities of life in the twenty-first century? It's easy to get stuck reacting to unhelpful patterns. And it's tempting to mirror the default values of safety, security, self-focus and material success that characterize our culture. We know that simplistic, rule-based and one-size-fits-all approaches won't work. Through this book we hope to invite you to explore a vision for family life that is imaginative, intentional, creative, soulful and globally aware.

HOW TO USE THIS BOOK

The chapters and exercises in this book can be worked through over eight weeks, but you may want to spend up to a month working with each chapter. If you are coparenting, if possible, work through these exercises together. You may even want to try reading each chapter out loud to one another and then discuss.

At the end of each chapter, you'll find a task checklist and a review of key competencies. Many people find the support of a small group helpful to enacting growth and change. An eight-week group learning guide is included in the back of the book for this purpose. Personally, we've found it helpful to revisit the themes, questions and steps explored in this book many times at various stages in the life of our family.

Wholeness and integration in our families are things we instinctually long for, but they don't happen automatically. It takes intentionality and effort to respond to the invitation to thrive. We invite you to practice using three pivotal tools as you work through the exercises in each chapter.

 REFLECTION

Have you ever said something to your child or spouse and then suddenly realized you sounded just like one of your parents? That's a small moment of self-awareness. When you're conscious of what you're saying and doing and aware of your internal state (your thoughts and feelings), you are more prepared to make intentional choices. "Do I want to keep saying things my parent said?"

Reflection can lead to self-awareness. It may seem scary, but we're inviting you to slow down and to risk taking a closer look at your patterns of action, your inner thoughts and the motives that shape how you show up in your family. Self-reflection can sometimes bring up feelings of shame or regret. That's a normal response but not the ultimate goal. Don't get stuck there. Be compassionate with yourself. It takes courage to observe yourself and ask questions such as "Why do I get so angry?" or "What do I really believe about success for my kids?" But it's worth the risk.

To help you cultivate greater self-awareness, we've included reflection questions in each chapter. When you come to a set of these questions, we encourage you to pause, reflect and journal your responses. At the end of each chapter you'll find a task checklist and a review of key competencies. *Keep a journal or notebook close by to respond to the questions in the chapters and to record your own developing family vision and values.* Later you may want to share these insights with your spouse or a supportive friend.

FAMILY MEETING

Family life can feel frustrating and fragmented when our actions aren't coordinated. Talking about your dreams and the important details of life together can help you build understanding and come to agreements with your spouse and other family members. Included in each chapter are questions to help you have these important conversations.

We suggest that you set aside a standing appointment of at least an hour each week to have purposeful conversations about your family. You may call this your weekly family meeting, which includes the adult decision makers in your household. As your kids get older, you'll want to have a short follow-up family meeting that includes them, to share and discuss joint decisions. If you're parenting solo, you'll want to enlist the support of a close friend, grandparent or parenting mentor to talk through conversation topics and your process.

Be prepared for the possibility that some of these conversations may be challenging or triggering. While Daniel and Rebecca were working through the steps explored in this book, they noticed that they were having more arguments than usual. Rebecca observed, "I think we had more conflict because we were talking about topics that are very close to us—conversations that we had been avoiding for a long time. Even though the process wasn't always fun, those conversations really helped us come to stronger agreements about how we wanted to move forward together." If a particular topic brings up a lot of tension, consider strategies that might help you communicate more calmly: have your conversation in a coffee shop, write out your thoughts to one another in the form of a letter, and, if necessary, return to the topic when you feel more ready. Some couples find that using one of these strategies helps them moderate their emotions and communicate more clearly and calmly.

Some couples struggle to talk, or one partner may be more willing than the other. If your gentle requests for conversation are repeatedly met with resistance or if your family is experiencing crisis, trauma or mental health challenges, seek the help of a couples' counselor before trying to work through the steps in this book together.

 ## WHOLE FAMILY ACTIVITY

Just as parents need focused time to connect and come to agreements, whole families are helped by having dedicated times to talk, listen, learn, laugh and take action. In each chapter, we suggest various family activities, which may include a table conversation or active project. This time will look different depending on the ages of your children.

Plan to spend about thirty to sixty minutes in focused conversation or activity and less time if your children are small. If focused conversation or activity is a new skill for your family, take time to introduce the practice in advance: "We're going to try some new things together over the next few weeks. I value your thoughts and perspectives and think your participation can help make us a stronger family."

Find a time when everyone is available and alert. If you have teenagers, ask them what time in the week they're willing to commit to while you're working through this book. Make it fun. To set the tone, serve a special meal, dessert or snack. With younger children, you may want to provide crayons and paper or quiet toys to keep their hands busy while they talk and listen.

These three tools—reflection, family meetings and whole family activities—are essential building blocks for an intentional approach to family life. Many of the tasks and practices we suggest are based on these tools. If you can establish these as regular habits in your family, they will help you move toward the intentional, integral and flourishing life together you desire.

THE BIRTH OF THIS BOOK

The action-reflection learning approach utilized in this book flows from our long-term work directing ReImagine, A Center for Integral

Christian Practice. We create workshop and retreat experiences that help people apply spiritual wisdom to everyday life, with a particular focus on the life and teachings of Jesus.

It may be helpful for you to know something about the context from which this book emerged. When our kids were one, two and three years old, we moved from a small town in Minnesota to an inner-city neighborhood in San Francisco, where we started Re-Imagine. Our family journey has been shaped by living in a racially, culturally, religiously and socioeconomically diverse environment where we had limited access to the social institutions that typically support families. When our kids were growing up, our neighborhood was largely characterized by poverty, gang violence and drug trafficking. Our goal was to prepare our kids to flourish faithfully in this dynamic environment, which motivated us to be all the more vigilant about creating a thriving family culture.

To help our kids survive and thrive, we have tried to create a family culture where we talk about everything, sharpen one another's thinking, live from strong beliefs and values, and respectfully engage the perspectives and experiences of others. We've tried to cultivate a similar space of inquiry with this book. Some readers may wish that we were more direct and explicit about what we think families should do or believe, or what they should tell their kids about X, Y or Z. Other readers may wish we were less prescriptive and specific in our examples and suggestions. We've tried not to assume too much about the reader, creating space with the questions and exercises in this book to help you clarify what you believe, desire and are ready to practice to help your family thrive.

You'll hear a lot stories about our family—and not because we are, by any stretch, the model of a thriving family. It's simply the family we know best, and some dynamics of family culture are only accessible to members of that particular family. We've tried to mine our family experiences and growth processes merely for illustrative purposes, without presuming they're normative.

KEEP IN MIND

Family thriving is about process, not perfection. When a vision for family thriving is presented, it can be tempting to compare yourself to that vision and feel judged. Try to resist those urges and impulses. The last thing you need is another message about how you're doing it wrong. Shame and "shoulds" aren't healthy or helpful motivators. You love your children and are trying to guide and provide for them in the best possible ways with the resources you have. You want to relate to your spouse and participate in the life of your family in beautiful ways. That's something to celebrate.

With this book, we simply want to help strengthen your skills for belonging and becoming. If reflection questions, intentional conversations and family activities are new for your family, the number and variety we suggest may feel overwhelming. Start with where you are, and take a new step. Don't feel like you have to do everything. At the end of each chapter, pause for a moment and ask, What am I being invited into? What new step are we ready to take as a family right now?

Family thriving is about both vision and action. Most of us tend to be either big-picture focused or practically oriented. If you're a practical person, you may read this book and gravitate toward ideas for new activities and practices. You may be a highly motivated person who makes lists and will attempt to do all of the activities. We've tried most of the practices included in this book, but we didn't begin all of them at once or continue them in every season of life. Practices and activities are useful if they help you get the intended results that support your goals; they are not an end in themselves. *Why* we do things—our motives and intentions—is as important as *what* we do. So if you tend to focus on activity, try to pay extra attention to sections that explore the "why" questions.

If you're a big-ideas person, you may find yourself reading with an eye for underlying principles and skimming over the practical examples. Push yourself to make connections between ideas and action, and move from thinking to doing. If you find yourself thinking, *That's a lame practice*, or *I'd never do that*, pay attention. Explore why you react to a particular topic or exercise. Resistance is often close to where we're being invited to grow and change. The practice you resist could be the one that proves to be the most transformational.

Family thriving takes cooperation and work. As human beings created in the divine image, we have a lot of power to decide how we will live and relate to one another. As a parent, you have the power and privilege of initiating the direction that your family takes. Your children, also, are full human beings, worthy of respect and dignity, who can participate in creating and enacting a culture of belonging and becoming.

Parents and kids together create the culture of a family. When kids feel like they have ownership and can participate in the process, they're more likely to get on board. This doesn't mean that kids get to decide everything (adults do have more wisdom and experience), but that their ideas and concerns are heard and considered. Together you can embrace the power to imagine, create and enact a culture of belonging and becoming.

Anything worth doing takes focus, and change requires attention. Over the years, we've been surprised by how much intentionality and effort are required to take new steps in our family. It never seems like a good time to change, and we've both faced internal obstacles. Lisa enjoys the agreements that come from having regular family meetings, but she sometimes dreads the process. Mark tends to propose big changes—such as "Let's start growing all of our own food"—that none of us has the bandwidth to accomplish. In retrospect, we've gotten more traction when we take smaller, more realistic steps, such as "Let's plant an herb garden."

At times we've felt discouraged when we've tried to make changes and then fallen back into old patterns. But we've learned that change is often gradual. As you seek to make changes, you will encounter obstacles. Don't be discouraged, make time in your schedule, and keep at it, knowing that your hard work will be rewarded.

AS STRONG AS A REDWOOD FOREST

For the past nineteen years, our family has lived in an old Victorian house in San Francisco. Our home, built in 1890, is made of first-growth redwood that was cut down in the days following the great California Gold Rush. Coastal redwoods (*Sequoia sempervirens*) are among the tallest and oldest trees on earth. Redwood trees can live for up to 2,200 years. So it's possible that the timber studs and siding on our house were part of a living tree during the life of Christ or the Holy Roman Empire. The boards are so strong they've outlasted the nails that held them together.

Trees and families have many similarities. It's not surprising that we often refer to our ancestors and ourselves as parts of a family tree, because trees are a symbol of life, rooted and unfolding through generations. Redwood trees grow in circles, called faerie rings, as the shoots of new trees sprout up rapidly around a dying parent plant. The details of how redwoods grow provide a helpful image for what a human family needs to thrive.

Receptive. Redwood trees require access to energy beyond themselves. They stretch out their branches to receive the nourishment of coastal fog, sunlight and rain. To thrive, human families need to develop receptivity to the light, energy and love of the Creator, discovering how we're connected to God's larger story. What kind of world is this? Who are we? Why are we here? Your family can cultivate awakening to God's care and the larger story we are all part of by embracing life-giving spiritual practices and making conscious ethical choices.

Rooted. Redwood trees grow with the rhythms and cycles of life. If you cut open a redwood, you'll discover tree rings, a record of time and seasons. Thriving families are rooted in healthy rhythms for living well together in time. Your family can enact household rhythms and policies that are life giving and that support your family's shared purpose.

Connected. Redwood trees grow together in circles connected by interlocking roots that protect them from high winds. The roots are shallow, so their strength comes from strong links with one another. Similarly, thriving families find ways to foster belonging and care, and they support one another through life's storms. Your family can develop skills to relate with love and respect and pursue healthy ways to connect, communicate, navigate conflicts and have fun.

Responsive. Redwood trees are resilient to threats and responsive to opportunities to grow. Their bark, which is highly tannic and fire-resistant, protects them from danger. For giant sequoias, a close relative to the redwood, fire is essential to their reproduction, releasing the seeds from which new life can grow. Similarly, thriving families are committed to helping one another develop and embrace the challenges and stages of life as opportunities for growth and change. Your family can embrace each person's belovedness, hold one another's brokenness and support one another in responding to the invitation to grow and change.

Resourceful. Redwood trees are a fruitful part of a larger living system. With their branches, they efficiently collect water from passing fog, and they absorb nutrients from the surrounding soil. They take only what they need to be sustained and also give back to the forest. Their fallen leaves provide nourishment to forest creatures, and their canopy creates a habitat for other plants, birds, insects and animals. Thriving families learn to see themselves as part of a larger economy of abundance and interdependence. Your family can live abundantly by using resources wisely and practicing gratitude, trust, contentment and generosity.

Productive. Redwood trees are constantly investing in the future. New seedlings often sprout from burls or roots at the base of a parent plant or fallen tree. One tree can produce six million seeds in a single year. A thriving family celebrates each person's uniqueness and supports the development of skills and capacities to serve others and pursue the greater good. Your family can flourish by learning to engage the needs and opportunities of our world.

Purposeful. Redwood trees know what their purpose is; it's encoded in their DNA. One dramatic difference between trees and people is that human families must make conscious choices to embrace a shared purpose. A thriving family knows what it's about. Your family can live from a deep sense of purpose and a positive vision of the future that you can articulate and use as a guide for decision making.

The first-growth redwood forests of the California coast are nearly gone. Ninety-five percent have been cut down, and those that remain thrive only because they are protected. It can seem like the ecology for family thriving is also threatened. In today's world, creating a thriving family culture requires vigilance and daily tending. What can you do to adapt, cultivate and protect family thriving in a changing landscape? You can (1) stop and reflect on what is and is not working, (2) explore new possibilities and (3) take new life-giving steps.

 REFLECTION

The family thriving self-assessment. Every family has strengths and growth areas. The following exercise is designed to help you celebrate places of strength and identify potential areas of growth in your family so you can take steps toward fuller flourishing.

Below are seven dimensions of family thriving. Read and respond to *each* statement, and circle the number that best reflects your current family experience—from 1, strongly disagree, to 5, strongly agree.

1. *Purposeful.* A thriving family lives from a deep sense of purpose and a positive vision of the future that it can articulate and use as a guide for decision making.

We have decided what to keep and what to leave behind from our families of origin.	1 2 3 4 5
We've thought critically about inherited and adopted family scripts.	1 2 3 4 5
We are able to talk about what matters most to us.	1 2 3 4 5
We share a positive vision of our future together as a family.	1 2 3 4 5
Our family has a shared purpose that we can articulate.	1 2 3 4 5

Total _____

2. *Rooted.* A thriving family enacts household rhythms and policies that are life giving and that support the family's shared purpose.

Our rhythm of life is sustainable and has space for work, rest, play and meaningful celebrations.	1 2 3 4 5
We have an effective venue and process for planning and decision making.	1 2 3 4 5
We have agreements about how tasks will be accomplished.	1 2 3 4 5
We're making conscious tradeoffs with our time and money to pursue what matters most.	1 2 3 4 5
We're intentional about the amount of time we spend in front of screens and engaged with entertainment and social media.	1 2 3 4 5

Total _____

3. *Receptive.* A thriving family cultivates awakening to God's care and the larger story we are all part of by embracing life-giving spiritual practices and making conscious ethical choices.

We explore and articulate our understanding of the larger story in open dialogue.	1 2 3 4 5
We have shared life-giving spiritual practices that help ground and sustain us.	1 2 3 4 5
We have a venue to sharpen our thinking and discuss values, ethics, beliefs and the important needs and opportunities in our world today.	1 2 3 4 5
We make shared choices about how to deepen the practice of our ethics and values.	1 2 3 4 5
To our best ability, we're living out our deepest values with consistency, and we're honest when we aren't.	1 2 3 4 5

Total _____

4. *Connected.* A thriving family relates with love and respect and pursues healthy ways to connect, communicate, navigate conflicts and have fun.

We spend time together doing activities we enjoy that help us feel connected.	1 2 3 4 5
We celebrate one another, express appreciation and say "I love you," and family members feel seen, heard and cared for.	1 2 3 4 5
We have shared rules of love and respect that govern how we treat one another.	1 2 3 4 5
We have effective tools for navigating conflict, making repairs, offering forgiveness and negotiating boundaries.	1 2 3 4 5
Our family can welcome and invite others into our lives, including relatives, friends and new family members.	1 2 3 4 5

Total _____

5. *Responsive.* A thriving family embraces each other's belovedness, holds their brokenness and supports their growth.

We're growing in awareness of our personal growth challenges, can share honestly with one another and support one another's steps of growth.	1 2 3 4 5
We identify and celebrate the gifts and limits of each family member's personality.	1 2 3 4 5
We understand what may be age and developmentally appropriate expectations for each member of our family.	1 2 3 4 5
We focus more on internal character development than external behaviors or just following the rules.	1 2 3 4 5
We're able to talk critically and compassionately about the aches and struggles of the human condition.	1 2 3 4 5

Total _____

6. *Resourceful.* A thriving family lives abundantly, using resources wisely and practicing gratitude, trust, contentment and generosity.

We live with a sense of abundance, rather than worry or fear, and we trust that what we need will always be provided.	1 2 3 4 5
We're grateful and content; we have just the right amount of possessions; and we are learning to distinguish between wants and needs.	1 2 3 4 5
We have clear financial goals that reflect our values as well as a yearly budget to guide our spending choices.	1 2 3 4 5
We actively teach younger family members how to handle money, and we model the wise use of financial resources.	1 2 3 4 5
We're making conscious efforts to be ethical and sustainable in our consumption and generous with our resources.	1 2 3 4 5

Total _____

7. *Productive.* A thriving family celebrates each person's uniqueness and supports the development of skills and capacities to serve others and pursue the greater good.

We help identify, nurture and celebrate the gifts of each family member and help each other imagine how our gifts and skills can best serve others.	1 2 3 4 5
We resource the development of skills and capacities to help family members make a meaningful contribution to society.	1 2 3 4 5
We model and teach the dignity and value of work, diligence and a job well done.	1 2 3 4 5
We are helping each other discover how to compassionately engage the great aches and opportunities in our world.	1 2 3 4 5
We take steps to practice compassion and serve together as a family.	1 2 3 4 5

Total _____

Calculate the totals for each dimension of family thriving. Identify and circle two dimensions of greatest strength and two dimensions where you most desire growth.

1. Purposeful	Growth	Strength
2. Rooted	Growth	Strength
3. Receptive	Growth	Strength
4. Connected	Growth	Strength
5. Responsive	Growth	Strength
6. Resourceful	Growth	Strength
7. Productive	Growth	Strength

Family meeting. Explore your family strengths and growth areas. Take turns sharing one family strength that you identified and why you see it as a strength. Then share a family growth area you identified and why you see it as a potential place of growth. If you're parenting solo, process this exercise with a trusted friend or relative.

As you talk, practice active listening. Look your partner in the eye, listen carefully to what they say, and reflect back what you hear to confirm your understanding. Do two rounds of sharing potential strengths and growth areas, and then identify one of two areas you both want to pay particular attention to as you work through this book. You may also want to discuss these questions:

- Where do we have the most agreement?

- Where do we vary in our responses, and what factors account for those differences?

- Are there any statements in the self-assessment that we want to highlight for further conversation?

WHOLE FAMILY ACTIVITY: CELEBRATE YOUR FAMILY

Choose one of the activities below to celebrate what you love about your family and to explore what a family is for.

Draw and talk. Bring out paper and crayons. Have each person draw a family portrait or a picture of you all doing something you enjoy. Then take turns describing your pictures to each other. You can use prompts like these: What do you like about our family? How does our family help you? How do we help others?

Play a game. Play a version of hot-and-cold. Ask each person to think of an object in your home that reminds them of one good thing about your family. Choose someone to start, and have them lead you all to the object by giving clues about who is moving closer or farther away. The person should say "hotter" when someone moves toward the item and "colder" when someone moves farther away. When the group has finally touched or guessed the chosen item, ask why it reminded that person of your family. Play until everyone's had a turn.

Then ask some questions to extend the conversation: What is your favorite thing about our family? What is our family really good at? What is a good memory you have of our family? When do you feel close to our family?

Take a trip down memory lane. Look through your family photos together, talking about the memories they bring up. Then ask each person to respond to one or more of these questions: What are some of your best memories of our family? What do you value about our family? When have you felt most connected? How has our family helped each other grow? How has our family been able to bless others?

A prayer for family thriving. You can use this prayer to focus your family meetings and activity times—or create your own prayer.

> Make our family a place of belonging and becoming:
> one in purpose, together in rhythm, united by a common story.
> Help us connect with love and respect,
> growing in wisdom, living abundantly and productively
>   seeking the greater good,
> so that our family, and every family on earth, can thrive.

CHAPTER TASK CHECKLIST

- Complete the Family Thriving Self-Assessment.

- Have a family meeting, and talk through the self-assessment.

- Pick one whole family activity to help introduce this learning journey to your kids.

2

A Thriving Family Carries Out Its Purpose

OUR FAMILY LOVES TO WALK and hike. Before our kids were born, Lisa had already walked them hundreds of miles. Mark cherished carrying the kids close to his chest in the baby carrier, so it was a sad day when they graduated to the stroller. By the time our kids were toddlers, they had learned to walk two or three miles at a stretch. Over the years, our feet have taken us to amazing places, including the streets of San Francisco, London, Paris and Tijuana, and along the spectacular trails of Yosemite, Zion and Yellowstone National Parks.

When our family walks, we usually have a goal in mind. We're on an adventure and going somewhere—to the park or museum, a *taqueria* or an incredible vista. Knowing the destination is especially helpful for those with shorter legs who have a hard time appreciating the simple goal of getting fresh air and exercise.

One hike we took when our kids were in grade school was especially memorable—mostly because we're grateful to have survived it. On the map of Joshua Tree National Monument, we noticed a one-and-a-half-mile trail out to an oasis called Forty-Nine Palms. Mark had hiked this trail before, and he thought it would be fun for the kids to see the contrast between the high desert heat and the cool shade of a spring surrounded by palm trees.

We packed water for each person, though not quite as much as the guidebook suggested, and set off. Soon we discovered that a mile and a half feels a lot farther when you're walking up and down hills at a high elevation in 113-degree heat. We couldn't wait to get to the shade of the oasis. But that season the oasis was a disappointingly muddy pond, teaming with tadpoles and swarming with bees and stinging flies. Then, partway back to the parking lot, we ran out of water. Our pace began to slow and stutter until, at the sight of yet another uphill ascent, the kids finally collapsed, one by one. Red-faced and nearing exhaustion, they began to moan, "Papa, how much farther is it to the car? When are we going to be there?" To keep them motivated, we talked up how refreshing the water would feel back at the hotel swimming pool and promised to buy whatever icy treat they wanted at the nearest gas station once we got back to Highway 62. No one moved.

Finally, Mark looked at the map, climbed to the top of the next hill, and exclaimed, "I can see the car! We're almost there!" With this news, the kids rallied. When *they* could see the car their pace quickened, and they ran ahead. Water never tasted so good, even though it was warm from sitting in the hot car. Icy treats had never been so delicious. We'd made it! As we slurped our slushies in the air-conditioning on the way back to Palm Springs, we reminisced about our hike.

"I thought we were going to die!" Isaiah exclaimed dramatically.

"We should have brought more water," Hailey stated matter-of-factly.

"Or started the hike earlier, before the sun was at its zenith," Noah added.

"That was my mistake," Mark said. "We will definitely pack more water next time. But you pushed through and made it. I'm really proud of you!"

Over the coming months and years, that Forty-Nine Palms hike became something of a legend in our family. We had gone on an adventure and, though it was challenging, had accomplished our goal together.

Family life is an epic adventure we embark on together, with many ups and downs and challenging conditions along the way. To be sustained and connected on this journey, we need a shared purpose—to know who we are, where we've come from, where we're going, what to carry and what to leave behind. *A thriving family lives from a deep sense of purpose and a positive vision of the future that it can articulate and use as a guide for decision making.* In this chapter, we'll explore steps for cultivating shared purpose as a family.

WHAT TO CARRY AND WHAT TO LEAVE BEHIND

In the family you're creating, you get to decide what you want to carry with you and what you want to leave behind from your family-of-origin experiences. Think about the values and traditions you've inherited that you would like to continue. Lisa wanted to bring along her family's Christmas celebrations and summer camping trips, and Mark wanted nightly table conversations, long walks and PPP (pizza, pop and popcorn movie nights). Perhaps you, like us, are trying to pack along as many of the qualities you appreciate from your family as you possibly can.

Some of us struggle to find much worth inheriting from our families of origin, or we feel there were major gaps. In those instances, we can borrow from the habits and traditions of families we admire. One person put it like this: "My family situation was extremely difficult, but other families welcomed me into their homes and lives. That love and care made me feel valued and had a powerful impact. I've borrowed many of their family traditions and made them my own."

Each of us also has inherited habits, attitudes and approaches to life that aren't helpful and that we'd like to leave behind. Daniel wants to leave behind the unpredictable anger and yelling that regularly occurred in his household. Rebecca wants to leave behind the coldness and demanding perfectionism that caused her pain. Even if there's a lot you appreciate about your family of origin, you'll likely make some choices that your parents or siblings won't understand. Every new family goes through this process of differentiation, though it isn't always easy.

Many of the things we want to unpack from childhood are obvious, while others seem to smuggle their way into our new families like unwanted baggage. Getting married, starting a family and sharing life so intimately can expose wounds and insecurities we weren't fully aware of. It's important to reflect on our family-of-origin experiences, because we tend to repeat or react to what we haven't examined.

MAKING PEACE WITH YOUR FAMILY INHERITANCE

We've found it helpful to talk extensively about our inherited family patterns and have, on occasion, read books or talked to a wise counselor to explore how we might make peace with our family inheritances. Leaving behind unwanted baggage from childhood or a previous relationship takes time and grace, but it's well worth the effort. And doing so helps you free up space to imagine and enact the family purpose you hope to pursue. Here are a few suggestions for making peace with your family inheritance.

See beyond all-or-nothing. Have you noticed the energy and intensity that often surfaces when the topic of parents comes up with close friends? Most of us have complicated feelings about the people who raised us. During the course of human development, it's natural to have inflated feelings about parents. For a season, our parents can do no wrong; they are perfect in our eyes because they're all we know of life. Even children who have been severely neglected or abused aggressively defend the reputations of their parents. There's a deep instinct inside us to honor and value where we come from, because where we come from says a lot about who we are. And we want to believe that we're beings of tremendous dignity, value and worth.

For many of us, a time comes—often in adolescence or early adulthood—when we begin to see our parents' faults and limitations, and we experience resistance to their authority. Suddenly, they can scarcely do anything right. Others of us want to hold on to and defend an idealized view of our parents. This can create an unhelpful dynamic in a couple's relationship where one person's family is characterized as "the good family" and the other as "the bad one." Hopefully we reach a point of maturity where we value the good while also acknowledging what was disappointing and painful. A healthy and mature understanding will lead us to hold the beauty and the pain of our family experiences in creative tension, as two parts of one whole.

Avoid determinism. Into the families we create we bring the legacy, gifts and wounds of previous generations and our memories of those who cared for us. Since many difficulties can be traced to early experiences, it's tempting to blame parents for whatever we don't like about ourselves. Research suggests that "individuals who grew up in families that were less functional and had more tension tend to have more difficulty managing the demands of their own marriages." It's important to note that we are shaped—not determined—by our family-of-origin experiences. How you process and interpret events from your past profoundly affects how you live in the present. It can take time to develop the wisdom and insight needed to distinguish between struggles that come from your family inheritance and those that are rooted in your personality, circumstances and life choices.

Develop compassion for your parents. Becoming a parent often brings new insight into family-of-origin experiences. Remember how you felt holding your child for the first time—that feeling of awe, utter delight and love you hardly knew existed? It can be an epiphany to realize that your own parent likely felt the same way about you. *All parents love and want the very best for their child.* Like you, your parents probably did the best they could with the resources they had.

It didn't take long after our children were born to realize that we were far from perfect parents. At times we've spoken harshly, disciplined rashly or acted from anger, impatience or distraction. The demands of adulthood and our personal challenges have made it hard to engage our kids consistently in the way we wish to. *Every parent makes mistakes and has limitations that inhibit their ability to provide what's needed.* Acknowledging your imperfections can help you empathize with your parents' limitations, forgive their mistakes and hope that your children will do the same for you.

We also recall a moment during the toddler years when each of our children began to express frustration, inner turmoil and resistance, despite our best efforts to show love and stay connected. *Every parent eventually learns that their love is not enough.* You can't protect your child from the loneliness and struggles inherent to the human condition—just as our parents couldn't protect us from these realities. But we can encourage each other to grow toward light and health.

The dynamics present in your family of origin may have connections to larger social and historical forces. Brian, who is second-generation Asian American, remembers his parents being busy, preoccupied and demanding, but with time he came to realize that those are common dynamics in first-generation immigrant and refugee families struggling to adjust to a new language and culture. Many people find it helpful to look at their family-of-origin experiences from the larger horizon of ethnic, cultural, religious, economic and historical circumstances. Mark's family was shaped by the Vietnam War, including the place and circumstances of his birth at a military base in Germany. Lisa's farming family was impacted by the farm crisis of the 1980s. Going further back, our grandparents were affected by the Dust Bowls and the Great Depression of the 1930s and by the religious fervor that swept through the Midwest during the Second Great Awakening. If you're able, it can also be helpful to learn about health histories and mental health patterns in your extended family;

these factors often run along family lines. Our parents and grand-parents and other caregivers experienced the unique challenges and opportunities of their time and place in history, and we will do the same.

It's no accident that all of the monotheistic religions teach the wisdom of honoring parents—those whose actions conceived, birthed and nurtured us. The Judeo-Christian instruction includes a promise: "Honor your father and mother so that you may live long." We honor our parents and ancestors by demonstrating appreciation for all they provided for us. We honor our parents by forgiving them their mistakes and limitations. And we honor our parents by seeking to improve on the good that was present in our family of origin.

Find ways to tell a cohesive story about your life. Sometimes we feel safe, loved and celebrated; other times we feel wounded, alone or abandoned. We develop beliefs and create a story about ourselves based on how we interpret these experiences.

From a neurological perspective, we don't actually remember what happened in our early lives. We remember our memories. This explains why you may have vivid memories of a dramatic event from childhood that other members of your family have little or no recollection of or that they perceived in a very different way. Our memories are colored by feelings and interpretations and by the ways we've practiced remembering. This suggests that there is some elasticity and flexibility to our memories. Clinical psychiatrist Daniel Siegel suggests that learning to tell a cohesive story about your life, including the difficult and challenging aspects, is critical to becoming an integrated self and a healthy parent—and, we would add, a healthy spouse as well.

We can learn to tell the stories of our lives as good stories that don't minimize or deny the pain or fixate on where we feel broken. One critical task is learning to see our life experiences within the larger context of the Creator's care, trusting that love has been with us through every moment of our lives. You can work to create a cohesive narrative about your life, one that owns the pain and affirms God's care. We see this process at work in the psychology of the psalms, where the poet experiences feelings of loss and abandonment while striving to affirm the promise of God's enduring love:

"Why have you forgotten me?
Why must I go about mourning . . . ?"
My bones suffer mortal agony
as my foes taunt me,
saying to me all day long,
"Where is your God?"
Why, my soul, are you downcast?
Why so disturbed within me?
Put your hope in God,
for I will yet praise [God],
my Savior.

Being raised in a family culture characterized by addiction, abuse or neglect may make it more difficult to trust that intimate relationships can be a place of safety and comfort. Knowing the ache that comes from a lack of attachment, an ancient psalmist wrote, "God sets the lonely in families." If you experienced a lack of natural attachment in your family of origin, you can pursue what psychologists refer to as "earned attachment": adult experiences of safety and connection that can help you learn to trust in the reality of love. In situations where parental interactions haven't been nurturing, it can help to explore questions such as:

- In addition to my family of origin, who are parent figures or caregivers that played a role in my life and helped me trust that love is real?

- Who are the people right now who help me know that I am loved?
- Where in my life do I see evidence that I am loved and cared for by a good Creator?

Michelle grew up in a family that struggled to thrive. Her parents split up when she was a toddler, and her mom developed what became a lifelong addiction to alcohol that contributed to poverty, neglect and abuse by successive boyfriends. This made Michelle feel abandoned and unlovable. In her early teens, a classmate invited her to church, and there she was welcomed into a new family, where she discovered language for the warmth of God that she had often felt, even in the darkest moments.

Michelle went on to college, got married and now has a growing family of her own. She says,

> Many people raised in environments like mine really struggle—but I believe that healing of those memories and experiences is possible. The Scripture "in all things God works for the good" is sometimes used as a trite response to deep pain, but I actually find it to be profoundly healing and true. This doesn't negate or dismiss the wounds and scars I have, but I've seen many of them turned for good.

Our family-of-origin experiences give us our first impressions of what God is like and the trust and hope that love is real. However, the love that parents and family can provide is never enough. Our experience of family sets us on the journey and search for a true parent and true home. Perhaps this is the greatest journey of our lives—to discover our connection to the ultimate reality, trusting that the universe is a safe place to be and embracing all that life brings. "Live in me. Make your home in me" is how Jesus described this invitation, affirming what the ancients knew: "Lord, you have been our dwelling place throughout all generations."

THE SCRIPTS THAT GUIDE AND SHAPE US

We are each guided by scripts that inform our goals and decisions about daily activities. They are the rails our lives run on. Often we develop these scripts based on values we've adopted from our family or culture, or in reaction to what we felt was missing or overemphasized. Your scripts are likely rooted in the particular longings of your personality and life experiences. Some scripts are very concrete: "I didn't get to play sports, but my kids are definitely going to be in Little League." Others reflect overall themes: "I didn't feel known or nurtured in my family, so I'm going to make sure my kids feel close and cared for."

The scripts we inherit aren't necessarily the ones that were intended. Justin grew up with parents who worked hard to provide him with a life of opportunity and financial security. They never would have said, "What's important in life is making lots of money and achieving in your career," but that's the unspoken impression he got from their actions. So he finds himself saying, "The family I help create is going to be about adventure and fun. Who cares about money!" Reflecting on his scripts, Justin made this observation, "So much of what I do as a parent is a negative reflex to what I experienced in my family. My hope is to find a positive family purpose and not just react to what I experienced as a kid. When I think about it, I am grateful for what my parents taught me; I just want there to be more balance."

In themselves, scripts aren't good or bad, right or wrong. But each script can have a negative impact if it leads to the neglect of other dimensions of family thriving. For instance, in our family, Mark tends to be driven by an intense sense of mission. He wants our family to be about a higher purpose. This is a good thing, but can sometimes lead him to take on too many commitments. Lisa, on the other hand, longs to feel close and connected to our kids. But she also recognizes that her desire for intimacy, if not kept in balance, can prevent her from empowering our kids to develop autonomy and responsibility. As you become more conscious of your scripts, you're better able to decide how you want them to guide your family's journey. Which of the scripts below do you most identify with?

The drive toward achievement: I want our family to be successful. Every person must learn how to be effective and productive, but it can be harmful if we measure success only by external outcomes and validation. Our goal can be helping one another identify the unique work we were made to do in the world. A better question than "Are we successful?" may be "Are we becoming the kind of people we were made to be?"

The drive toward security: I want our family to be safe and protected. The world can feel like a scary place, and it's every parent's desire to create a safe and nurturing environment for their child. But if we're too careful, we can let our worries and fears prevent our children from experiencing the small dangers and discomforts that can help them gain the competence and confidence to navigate larger challenges. We grow by taking risks and learning from our mistakes.

The drive toward moral perfection: I want our family to do what's right. We all want our kids to make good moral and ethical choices and to avoid harmful decisions. The question is whether this is best achieved by focusing on external behavior and conformity or by helping our kids develop the critical thinking and internal character to be governed by a deeper moral compass.

The drive toward individuality: I want people in our family to be free to express themselves. It's important for children to develop autonomy and volition, gaining confidence in their desires; but this doesn't mean they always get what they want. We were designed to find our deepest satisfaction in relationships of mutuality, respect and self-giving love, which requires balancing individual preferences with the needs and feelings of others and focusing on the common good.

The drive toward the good life: I want our family to have fun and enjoy the best. As parents, we naturally want to give good gifts to our children, providing them with resources and experiences they enjoy. Yet a preoccupation with material goods and consumptive experiences can distract from what's important. The question is, how much is enough, and what actually brings satisfaction?

The drive toward family intimacy: I want our family to feel close and connected. We're made to experience intimacy and connection, but when taken to the extreme, the desire for belonging can inhibit becoming. At its best, family provides a sense of safety from which family members are launched into growth, purpose, individual identity and interdependence.

The drive toward a mission: I want our family to be about a higher purpose. It's important for a family to have a purpose beyond itself. But when the mission is pursued at the expense of family members' well-being, this drive can be a problem. At times the mission may need to be put on hold to care for family concerns, because our family members are as important as the causes we serve—and no less worthy of our time, care and attention.

The drive toward survival: I have to manage pressing concerns. Many of us will experience a crisis during the course of family life that taxes our resources and exceeds our abilities to cope (financial difficulties, divorce, death or disability, physical or mental health issues). As we face these emergencies, it can be challenging to find a balance between the urgencies of the moment and the ongoing needs of family members. If we get stuck in fight-or-flight responses, family life can be characterized by chaos and alarm. Finding external support, internal strength and perspective can help us navigate these times with resiliency.

You may find it helpful to spend some time exploring the potential benefits and shadows of the scripts you most closely identify with. When you're aware of what's guiding your decisions, you're more prepared to make conscious, life-affirming choices.

 REFLECTION: EXAMINE YOUR FAMILY-OF-ORIGIN EXPERIENCES AND SCRIPTS

Important steps in activating your family purpose are (1) appreciating the gifts and challenges of your family inheritance, (2) seeking to understand, forgive and honor your parents and (3) deciding what you want to carry with you and what you want to leave behind. Considering the family situation that you were raised in, spend twenty to thirty minutes writing your responses to the following journal prompts. At your next family meeting, share what you discover in your reflection.

Family inheritance.

- What qualities, values and traditions from your family of origin do you hope to carry with you into the family you're creating?

- What do you admire in other families that you would like to emulate?

- What are the patterns, habits and approaches to life from your family of origin that you would like to leave behind?

Coming to peace with your family-of-origin experiences.

- Where are you in the ongoing process of understanding your parents' limitations and forgiving their mistakes?

- What are the larger historical events and social dynamics that shaped your family-of-origin experience?

- Are you able to tell a cohesive story about your life? What memories are still in need of healing?

Your personal scripts.

- What scripts from your family of origin are you repeating or reacting to?

- Which two or three scripts are the dominant drivers in your approach to family and parenting? What are the potential benefits and shadows of these scripts?

- How are the scripts that drive you similar to or different from those of your spouse or coparent? Are there ways that you balance out each other's tendencies?

WHERE ARE WE GOING TOGETHER?

Have you ever been part of a group that can't decide where to go or what to do? It can be very frustrating. Having a clear purpose becomes crucial when two or more people travel together. Creating a family purpose agreement will help your family build a shared identity and vision. It can also provide a mechanism for focusing your energy and making important decisions. To say it another way, a family purpose agreement gives you a reliable compass for navigating the terrain of life together.

Before we got married, the two of us spent a lot of time talking about our shared dreams. We were drawn together by a common purpose and values. As we looked into the future, our vision was somewhat cloudy. As our kids came along, we found ourselves overwhelmed by very specific decisions and responsibilities. Is it time to get a new job? What about graduate school? How long do we want to stay living here? Where do we see ourselves in five or ten years?

As we mentioned in the first chapter, it felt like competing demands were pulling us apart and making our lives disjointed. We were tired, busy and distracted. It was time to revisit the big questions again and make our vague common direction more explicit.

One night, after putting Hailey to bed, we sat down to craft a formal family purpose agreement. We spent some time praying and then brainstormed a two-page list of values and potential goals based on questions such as "What matters most to us?" and "What do we want to be about together in life?" Then we tried to distill our brainstorm into a few essential statements that looked something like this:

As a family, with God's help, we strive to

- know and love God
- nurture healthy family relationships
- offer hospitality and care, especially to those who struggle and suffer

- use our gifts to serve
- live gratefully, creatively and sustainably

It was energizing to articulate and affirm what mattered most to us. We were so excited by this newfound clarity that we created a poster of our agreement and hung it in the kitchen, on the bathroom mirror and on the front door of our house. For the next few weeks, we read it aloud together every night at dinner. As we began using it to orient our family meetings, it became a compass to guide us over the coming years.

For us, getting more clarity about short-term decisions prepared us to consider what the longer future might look like. We had imagined living in an urban neighborhood in a global city, working side by side to create community, love our neighbors and help people experience greater wholeness in their lives. But here we were living in the country, miles from Mark's job and separated for most of the day. How could we get from the life we had to the life we imagined?

Over the next few months we spent many hours talking and praying through steps we could take, like saving money, shifting careers and adjusting some of our expectations about what life might look like for our family. Moving to a big city and starting new work seemed like a big risk. Might it be possible to live into our dreams and ideals and thrive as a family? We decided that if we had the courage to live the life we felt called to, then we could trust that this was also a life where our kids would flourish. What if our kids would best be served if they saw us being fully alive?

When our children were one, two and three, we launched into what would prove to be one of the greatest adventures of our lives. We relocated to San Francisco, bought an old rundown house in a struggling neighborhood and began the journey to the life we have today. Eventually we started a nonprofit and began launching programs to create community, make beauty, serve needs and live out our deepest values. Our kids have been our partners in this adventure, and our home has been the center of our shared life and work. In a typical week twenty or thirty people might walk through the door. If you stopped by you might meet a guest who is currently sleeping on our couch, find a group of high school students learning chemistry together at the kitchen table or discover a group of university students working on a community art project in our backyard. We do all of this in eleven hundred square feet that is a school, an office, a community meeting space and home to our family of five. Clarifying and articulating our family purpose agreement was an important step that launched us into this adventure. It hasn't always been easy, and we've often gone off course, but our family purpose agreement has been like a compass pointing us to true north.

 ## FAMILY MEETING: CREATE A FAMILY PURPOSE AGREEMENT

The particulars of your family vision might be very different from ours, and that's okay. Every family is unique. Taking the time to develop a shared purpose agreement will help you live more fully into your dreams and values.

Many families know the benefits of creating a shared purpose agreement.

- The process of creating your purpose agreement can help you get on the same page about what matters most. There are an infinite number of things you could do with your time and energy. A family purpose agreement can help you develop common priorities and a greater sense of unity and solidarity in your activities.

- A family purpose agreement can help you remember why you are choosing your daily activities and priorities. In the midst of long work hours, 3 a.m. feedings, dirty diapers and piles of laundry, it is easy to lose perspective. Life can start to feel like an endless to-do list. Seeing the connections between mundane tasks and deeper goals gives them new meaning that can help you stay motivated. Lisa remembers reminding herself, *I'm giving this care and attention to dishes, food, diapers and story time because these people matter and this is what I can do to care for them today.*

• A family purpose agreement can help you make conscious choices about how you spend your time. When invitations and new opportunities arise, you'll have a list of values and priorities in place that can help you decide whether to say yes or no. You can feel good about your scheduling choices when you see how they support and align with your family purpose.

• A family purpose agreement can help you navigate big decisions and empower you to take tangible new steps.

From our observations, couples and families who can clearly articulate a shared vision and purpose are more likely to thrive in their relationships. It's never too early or too late to consider larger questions of meaning and purpose.

A family purpose agreement isn't something that one person can dictate or impose on other members of the family. That approach just won't work. But, as a parent, you have the power to initiate the process, inviting family members to shape and contribute to a shared vision and common understanding. While there will likely be some overlap between your personal goals and your family purpose agreement, they aren't synonymous and won't be in total agreement, because one is individual and the other is what you share in common as a family.

When new parents Dave and Krissy came to us for advice about family life, our first question was "What is your family purpose?" Their response was "Umm, we're not sure we have one." After further consideration, they came to realize that they had a shared purpose; it just hadn't been clearly articulated. Most families have some sense of their purpose, but until it's spoken, it's difficult to use as a guide for navigating life and making decisions.

Over the next few months, Dave and Krissy created a family purpose agreement that's now their shared compass. Here's what they came up with:

- *Generosity.* We live with open hands and an open heart and give freely from abundance.

- *Integration.* Our work, play and family life are connected with our neighborhood, faith community and care for the earth.

- *Wholeness.* We cultivate intimacy with God and each other and live into our identity as beloved in both our beauty and our brokenness.

- *Curiosity.* We engage others, God and the world with a spirit of openness and adventure.

- *Celebration.* We are each other's best cheerleaders, and we intentionally and spontaneously cultivate joy in our family and community.

Dave and Krissy's family purpose agreement is poetic, which fits their interests and personalities. But a simple list of words can be just as useful. Melissa and her ex-husband, Michael, coparent two high-needs children who are on the autism spectrum. "Because of our challenges," Melissa says, "our family purpose agreement is focused on boundaries and basics: Pray. Be kind. Show respect. Be grateful. Love God and people. Work on yourself so you have something to give."

What you want is something succinct, but adequately descriptive and memorable. Don't get hung up on trying to say it perfectly or capture every nuance. If your kids are at an age that they can participate, you'll eventually want to invite them into this process, but it can be helpful to think about your family purpose first as adults. Take time to pray, reflect and discuss what matters most to you. Practice good brainstorming, which means focusing on the future, staying positive and not editing each other's ideas.

Below are some key life dimensions you may want to address in your family purpose agreement. Use these questions to spark your initial brainstorming conversation:

- *The larger story.* What do our faith, beliefs and experiences tell us about what is of ultimate importance? Why are we here? What makes life meaningful? What is the purpose of human existence? Is there a Scripture that speaks to us about these questions—for example, Scriptures about loving God and neighbor, seeking God's kingdom, and doing justice, loving mercy and walking humbly?

- *Relationships.* How do we want to care for and nurture one another? Who else are we committed to traveling with through the seasons of life (grandparents, aunts and uncles, cousins, friends, our faith community, our neighborhood)?

- *Vocation.* How do we want to be of use in the world? What is our unique work, contribution or calling as a family?

- *Passions.* Out of all that we could care about, what are we especially passionate about? How are we uniquely wired to seek the greater good?

- *Values.* What are the principles and ideals that we want to guide us?

After you've had a chance to dream together and capture a substantial list of possibilities, try to distill your family's purpose into five to seven key words or phrases. They should be broad enough to span several stages of family life and specific enough to be evocative. Write these in your notebook.

As a side note, some couples find it challenging to have deep conversations about what matters most, and one person may be more interested than the other. Often in relationships one person initiates while the other responds, but lack of initiation doesn't necessarily indicate a lack of interest or willingness. Perhaps a different way of approaching the conversation is needed. Are you invested in a particular outcome, or are you open to other perspectives? If you have different ideas about what's important, start by focusing on areas where you do have agreement. What values and goals do you share? Perhaps there's a larger value or principle that can encompass what you both desire. Take time to discover a style of communication that works for both of you.

 ## WHOLE FAMILY ACTIVITY: INVITING YOUR KIDS TO ENGAGE WITH YOUR FAMILY PURPOSE

Once you've brainstormed a family purpose agreement, engage your kids in the process by inviting them to contribute language and ideas toward the final product, so they feel ownership. They'll likely come up with a list similar to yours. If your children help shape your family purpose, they're more likely to be invested and excited about living into it. As you share a summary of your brainstorming, give them an opportunity to name, in their own words, what they believe is most important to your family. Below are some ideas for doing this at various ages and stages of family life.

Let's play family. Use your family's stuffed animals, dolls or action figures to play, pretend and talk about family purpose. Have each person pick a toy that they will role play with and narrate as you play together. Offer some prompts, such as

- Let's play family.

- Who's the mom, and what does Mom do in the family?

- Who's the dad, and what does Dad do in the family? Who else is in the family, and what do they do?

- What's the family doing?

- Where are they going?

During your play, introduce themes from the five to seven statements you brainstormed. For example, "This family loves each other. How do they show it?" "This family goes on adventures. Where are they going?"

Go on an adventure. For this activity, choose a fun destination in your neighborhood, a park, an open space, a library or a child-friendly café or grocery store. Invite your children to decide what route you'll take to get there. Do whatever drew you to this destination, and when you're ready, explain that being a family is an epic adventure. Then invite the family to brainstorm about that adventure. "Let's think about where we want to go as a family and how we want to get there."

Bring markers and paper for everyone to draw on. On one sheet of paper, write the following fill-in-the blank questions. On another sheet, write the words that they brainstorm in response.

Two things that are important to our family are _____ and _____.

Our family is made to _____ together.

We live out what is important to us by _____.

When people think of our family, a word that we hope they use to describe us is _____.

The unique job God has for our family is _____.

We want our family to feel _____.

With others, we want to be _____.

Then have each person draw a picture of what they imagine your family will be like and feel like in ten, fifteen or twenty years. Take turns explaining your pictures.

Present and future. With teens, you may have just a few more years in the same household together to live out a common purpose. Have a conversation about what your family journey has been like so far and where you hope to go together in the future. You may want to have a whiteboard and markers on hand to document the process with words and pictures.

Discuss the present together. Use the questions below as conversation starters.

- What do you think our family is known for?

- What do we value, and how do you think we live out what we say is important?

- How can we care for and support one another right now?

- What is our work to do, and how do we do it?

Imagine the future together. Sometimes it's good to remember that we're going to be part of our families for the rest of our lives. You can help each other envision a positive future together. Invite each person to imagine how you may be a family in twenty, thirty or forty years, and then share some of your hopes and dreams. Below are some examples from conversations we've had in our family:

"Someday you'll make a great husband and caring father. If you have a child someday, I'll be so excited to hold that little one in my arms."

"When I have a family, I hope you'll live close by and help me teach my kids."

"Maybe someday we'll buy some property together or start a nonprofit or business."

"When we're older and have our own families, I hope all of us can get together once a year at a cabin or the beach."

"When you were young, I changed your diapers. And someday, when I'm older, you might have to change mine."

After sharing what you imagine and hope for, ask each other this question: What do we need to do now in order to make those good hopes and visions for the future real?

AFFIRMING YOUR FAMILY'S PURPOSE

After getting input from your kids, finalize a family purpose agreement and find ways to regularly remind each other of it. Make a poster or display your purpose agreement on a bulletin board or chalkboard. Or make an art piece that communicates your agreement, using words or symbols to illustrate key points. Display what you create near your dinner table or another place where you will see it often.

Some families memorize and regularly recite Scripture passages that embody aspects of their shared purpose. For generations, in Jewish tradition, families have sung the Shema together as a way of orienting to their core purpose: "Hear, O Israel, the LORD our God, the LORD is one. Love the LORD your God."

Or you could craft your own family prayers. Our family created a prayer to say together based on the meanings of our kids' middle names. We repeat this prayer three times, each time using another one of their names (Agape, Joy and Shalom). For example:

Love in me.
Love between.
Love to our house.
Love to our neighbors.
May your love be upon us today.
We will speak love.
We will walk in love.

A CHILD'S TAKE ON FAMILY PURPOSE, BY HAILEY JOY SCANDRETTE

Another word for purpose is *mission*. The first thing I think of when I read the word *mission* is how much I wanted to be a spy when I was little. Now, before you decide this is wholly unrelated to the concept of setting values-based intentions for yourself and your family, hear me out.

From about age seven to age eleven, I thought that being a spy was as cool as life could get. I would put on silver plastic pants that I thought were the epitome of cool, a lavender turtleneck that I had cut the sleeves off of and a pair of purple sunglasses. (Every good spy needs a uniform.) I would grab a small notebook and sit on my bed, taking notes on passersby like Harriet the Spy.

Every so often my adventures in espionage took a more exciting turn in the form of "missions." In the weeks leading up to Christmas, my brothers and I would engage in covert operations. The mission: make the target's day better. For that person, I'd sneak chocolate under their pillow, leave affectionate notes, do chores or throw a surprise tea party complete with snacks and attended by dinosaurs and American Girl dolls.

Even when playing pretend or planning silly surprises for one another, we were aware that our purpose was to love others and to contribute to their well-being. I don't know if we were explicitly told as young children that part of our family's purpose was to love one another and those outside our family through generosity and hospitality. But it's clear our parents had a cohesive vision for the kind of family they wanted us to be, which they modeled so clearly that we picked up on it.

As an adult, I'm very grateful that the concept of having a purpose in life was so present in my family. It gave me a framework for developing a clear, values-based vision for the kind of life I want to have and the kind of person I want to be. Even when the details of career, education, relationships, etc., are up in the air, I can always ground myself by keeping my purpose in sight.

CHAPTER TASK CHECKLIST

- Reflect on your family-of-origin experience and scripts.
- Develop a family purpose agreement.
- Do an activity that invites your kids to engage with your family purpose.

REVIEW OF KEY COMPETENCIES

Purposeful. A thriving family lives from a deep sense of purpose and a positive vision of the future that it can articulate and use as a guide for decision making.

- We have decided what to keep and what to leave behind from our families of origin.
- We've thought critically about our inherited and adopted family scripts.
- We're able to talk about what matters most to us.
- We share a positive vision of our future together as a family.
- Our family has a shared purpose that we can articulate.

A Thriving Family Finds Its Rhythm

LOOKING BACK THROUGH YEARS of family photos, we see how the kids have grown, the way clothing styles have changed and how much older (and wiser?) we look now. You may be surprised by how many of the pictures show us playing music or dancing together. We weren't immune to the tendency to let movies or TV be our entertainment, but once in a while we got up the courage to make our own fun.

When friends came over, we would grab a violin, guitar, cello or pots and pans and have a jam session, or we'd clear away the furniture and have an impromptu dance party. Sometimes the kids put together elaborate dance routines to perform. Isaiah, in particular, had some amazing moves and developed what he called "the butt dance." He wasn't afraid to shake it, and we have the footage to prove it. There were even times when we rented out a dance hall and invited other families to get their groove on. Mark set up a sound system, Hailey and her friends created a playlist, and then moms and dads and kids of all ages—and sometimes grandpas and grandmas, too—would dance the night away.

When it comes to music or dancing, not everyone has the same skill, but if you can catch the rhythm, you're welcome to join in. Think for a moment about your favorite song. The rhythm may not be the first thing you notice, but it sets the time and drives the song along. The repeating pattern of sounds and spaces helps the musicians play in harmony with one another. They can play different instruments and notes, and as long as they're in the same time and key the results are harmonious. The rhythm is a standard the musicians have agreed to, beyond their individual preferences, that helps them play well and make beautiful music together. When they don't follow the same rhythm, the consequence is chaos and cacophony.

Family rhythms are shared agreements about how a family spends its time. It's bigger than any one member's desires; it's a standard tempo all surrender to and abide by. That rhythm provides the pace and dance steps to help you move through life together without crashing to the floor or stepping on each other's toes.

In the last chapter, we invited you to create a family purpose agreement to express what matters most to you. Shared rhythms are how that purpose can be lived out in the details of daily life. *A thriving family enacts household rhythms and policies that are life giving and that support the family's shared purpose.* In this chapter, we'll explore ways your family can be rooted in life-giving rhythms together.

ESTABLISHING LIFE-GIVING RHYTHMS

Life flows in cycles and rhythms. The sun rises and sets each day. The seasons have a rhythm that moves between dormancy and harvest. The body has its cycle of wakefulness and sleep, along with fluctuations in hormones and metabolism. In addition to the natural cycles of the earth and our bodies, we can create life rhythms that help us move in a good and orderly direction together.

As human beings, we thrive on rhythms: regular and repeated pockets of time spent on specific activities in our days, weeks, months and years. When we repeat behaviors, neural pathways are strengthened so certain activities become automatic. Our patterns of behavior can develop haphazardly, or we can consciously choose them. It's a lot easier to make good choices ahead of time, rather than in the heat the moment. Without intentionally chosen rhythms, we're prone to let the urgent or compulsive drive how we spend our time.

Rhythms are good habits we create to allow our deepest values to shape the cadence of our lives. Even Jesus lived in pockets and patterns of time, with parts of the day designated for solitary contemplation, public engagement and private time with his disciples. St. Paul urged his listeners to pay attention to their life patterns, being careful how they spent their time, "not as unwise, but as wise, making the most of every opportunity."

Let's face it; in a family there's a lot to juggle. You have to decide how to care for kids and connect as parents. Who will cook or clean? When will you shop, exercise, do home repairs and pay taxes? The two of us gradually realized that to live out our family purpose effectively, we needed a shared rhythm of life that really worked for us. As excited as we were about our shared purpose agreement, we realized it would be meaningless if it didn't translate into how we spent our time. The calendar doesn't lie. You can say you have a certain purpose, but your schedule reveals what you really believe is important.

It has helped us to adopt rhythms for the days, weeks and seasons that prioritize what we believe matters most. We try to give the most important activities designated time slots. We decided that, at a minimum, we needed protected times to connect as a couple and as a family, to complete work and household tasks, to pursue rest and self-care and to share our lives with others. When our kids were small, we began playing with a weekly rhythm that would help us do this. Thursday night became Dad and Kid Night so that Lisa could get space to herself. Friday night became family night, when we swam at the YMCA, watched a movie or played games at home. Saturday became our chore day, the time when we did yard work, deep cleaning and home maintenance. Saturday night was our date night. If we could find a babysitter, we went out; otherwise we relaxed together at home after putting the kids to bed. And Sunday nights became our hospitality night, when we invited a group of high school students to hang out at our house. It also helped us to have designated times during the week for a family meeting and one-on-one time with each child. Establishing these shared rhythms protected time for what we felt was most important.

The predictability of shared rhythms can create security, accountability and anticipation. Having a set time for certain tasks can help you follow through, even when you don't feel like it. If you always pick up toys or do family chores at a certain time, your kids will come to expect it, and they may even remind you if you forget. Regularity can also reduce the tendency to resist or complain.

When we were young parents, a mentor encouraged us to establish consistent, fun family activities that our kids could count on. After our move to California, we discovered Linda Mar, a quiet beach fifteen minutes from our house. We would take the kids there on sunny afternoons, packing a picnic or Chinese takeout. We always set up in the same spot by a weathered log. Nineteen years later, we're still going to that spot. It's our place to relax and connect in nature, and every time we go it reinforces a lifetime of positive memories.

Some rhythms reveal their power only over time. One of our enduring rhythms is eating together and having table conversations. Many of our dinnertimes are uneventful. But once in a while, something magical happens. We laugh hysterically, have that important conversation or a tender moment, and feel like we really belong to one another. Those cherished and unforgettable moments are made possible by the regular practice of showing up to the ordinary.

To some, the ordinary and predictable might sound boring compared with the fun and excitement of the spontaneous. But there's a surprising paradox. Consistent rhythms actually provide security and grounding that allow greater risks. As Pablo Picasso once famously said, "You have to learn the rules before you can break them."

CREATING FAMILY RHYTHMS

Daily, weekly and seasonal rhythms help us connect, care for one another and accomplish the good we've been prepared to do. Chosen rhythms are an important way to put your family purpose and values into practice. Your rhythms don't have to follow a prescribed pattern or be like anyone else's, but you want them to be mutually agreed upon and intentional. Here are some time-tested rhythms that have helped many families dance well together.

Daily rhythms.

Family meals. Eating together is a natural place to connect, tell stories, pray, share Scripture and have important table conversations. Some families also have a special weekly meal like Saturday morning pancakes, taco night or Sunday dinner.

Bedtime. The quieter moments at the end of the day can be a good space to read a story, talk, cuddle, reflect on highs and lows or pray about concerns. You can even maintain bedtime rituals when a parent is away, using a phone or video conference service to read stories or say good night.

Get outside. Going to "the park in the dark" was a favorite evening adventure when our kids were small. Getting active in fresh air away from screens is a great way to relax, have fun and connect.

Chores. Working together fosters camaraderie, teaches valuable skills and provides time together as you do what needs to be done. Talk while you work. With guidance, even small kids can help prepare meals or clean. Turn on the music and have a cleaning blitz to see how much you can accomplish in a certain number of minutes.

Weekly and monthly rhythms.

Family fun time. Consider creating expectation around a weekly family fun time. Some families pick a night of the week to eat pizza, share a movie or play games. Choose an activity your family enjoys, and relax together.

Faith community and sabbath. In addition to regular participation in a faith community, many families are discovering how helpful it can be to set aside a day or part of a day to rest, reflect and reconnect as a family. Some families make this a screen-free and device-free day.

Parent date time. Nurturing your romantic relationship can build intimacy that also provides security for your kids. Schedule regular times to enjoy a meal, a walk and a conversation. Some couples even find it helpful to schedule times for physical intimacy. Your date time doesn't have to be extravagant to be meaningful. We know families who swap childcare or create a babysitting pool so that many parents can have an affordable night out. Even if you spend your date time at home after the kids are in bed, you can make it special.

Parent-kid dates. You may want to schedule one-on-one time with each of your children. Go out together and do something you both enjoy. For years, Mark and Noah had a standing date on Saturday mornings, eating pastries and drinking coffee at a neighborhood cafe. Krissy and her son Everett have a weekly "Boba and Books" date: tea and a snack at their local bookstore.

Parent solo time. You don't have to be together constantly to thrive as a family. You may need regular alone time to recharge, and this can be a great opportunity for your children to spend special time with their other parent or a grandparent. Our kids always looked forward to Dad and Kid Night. Even when they were small, we wanted to provide each other with extended space for reflection and solitude, so every few months one of us would care for the kids while the other parent took a twenty-four-hour silent retreat.

Reentry rituals. If you're part of a family where a parent often travels for work, it can be helpful to create rituals around departures and reentry, such as a special meal with Mom when she gets back from her business trip or a small gift Dad brought back from the city he visited.

Seasonal rhythms.

Vacations. Traveling together away from your usual surroundings can help you learn, relax and connect in fresh ways. Camp, stay at a cabin in the mountains or explore a new city together.

Holidays. Create meaningful holiday traditions. Decide what you want holidays to mean to your family, and set your own expectations about gifts and activities that emphasize time together.

Birthday celebrations. Birthdays are a chance to remind the person being celebrated that they are loved and important. Let the birthday person choose a meal and activities for the day. Give them breakfast in bed. If it's a child, tell stories of their birth. Look at old photographs. Have everyone share what they appreciate about that person.

Contact with extended family. Building bonds with cousins, aunts, uncles and grandparents helps us appreciate the larger heritage of family. You may want to plan for regular times when you visit or welcome relatives and friends into your home. If they live far away, schedule times when you call or write.

Community service. Families are enriched by finding ways to serve together in their community. You may consider visiting an elderly neighbor, volunteering at a food pantry or helping with a park cleanup project. Even young kids love helping and meeting new people—and they can learn about compassion and citizenship through your example.

A rhythm isn't fixed; it can be improvised. Sometimes a family rhythm needs to change, because in a new stage or season it's no longer helpful or other priorities surface. Don't feel like you have to stick with something that isn't working anymore. A rhythm that's helpful with small children may not work with preteens or teens. You can build a large body of rhythms to draw from and choose those that best fit current needs and realities. The rhythms of your family can adapt and be flexible while still reflecting your purpose and values.

 ## FAMILY MEETING: IDENTIFY RHYTHMS THAT SUPPORT YOUR FAMILY PURPOSE

Take time to discuss rhythms you have in place as well as one or two new rhythms you'd like to enact in order to pursue what matters most to your family. Try not to add so many new rhythms that they become difficult to sustain. Start with a few essential rhythms, and slowly build from there. Reevaluate your rhythms regularly.

Here are some questions to consider as you identify and discuss your family rhythms. Record answers in your notebook.

- What rhythms already help us enact our family purpose?

- When and how during the week will we connect as adults, as a family and as parent and child?

- What are one or two new rhythms we would like to try in the coming months?

- What will help us remember and maintain the shared rhythms we're committed to?

When you establish daily, weekly, monthly and seasonal rhythms that reflect your values, those values become part of the music of your life. In this process, we "do not *merely* look out for [our] own personal interests, but also for the interests of others." At times we do something for someone we love that isn't very important to us. If I'm looking out for you, and you're looking out for me, we can relax and not defend our own needs and desires so stringently.

This is part of creating beauty in the dance of life together. By making and keeping agreements about rhythms and chores, we build an atmosphere of trust, care, love and responsibility in our homes. Like dancers on the stage, we get better at it with practice and learn to improvise new steps through the passages of life.

CREATING A VENUE FOR MAKING DECISIONS TOGETHER

Talking about your family purpose and identifying shared rhythms can be exciting. But perhaps, like us, you've discovered that the hardest part is following through on those good intentions. One couple confessed, "We can come up with a great vision and plan, and we forget about it in, like, five minutes—or we'll start a new rhythm that only lasts for two days." The competing demands of family life can make it difficult to follow through and stay on track with the purpose and priorities you've identified. Having a regular venue for checking in on goals and making decisions can help you keep to your life-giving rhythms.

We've found that when we don't make time to check in on our priorities, we end up losing track of our goals. Or the need for a decision erupts at an urgent or inconvenient moment. Mark might bring up our finances over family dinner, or Lisa might raise a parenting issue when we're out on a date, or one of us might bring up the sink full of dirty dishes while we're in the bedroom, disrupting planned romantic activities.

We've discovered that it works best for us to have a dedicated weekly space to talk about the many important facets of our shared life, ideally at a time when we aren't distracted or exhausted. We call this our family meeting. When our kids were small, the best time to have our family meeting was on a weekend morning. We'd pack up the kids in strollers or backpacks and walk to a park. The kids were usually content for a stretch of time while we walked, and we would often all play together at our destination. At other times, it worked to have our family meeting on a weekend night after the kids were in bed, or on a long car ride while they were napping.

In chapter 1, we introduced the family meeting as a key practice for working through the exercises in this book. We recommend you continue this practice as a pivotal rhythm that can help you keep momentum with your good vision and dreams. Having a weekly or regular family meeting can help you

- align your time with your family's purpose agreement
- create space for making important decisions and for problem solving
- increase communication and get on the same page about the important tasks of life
- stay on track with your goals and priorities
- celebrate progress and growth

When we first started having family meetings, we created an agenda each time. Gradually we identified this list of topics we wanted to discuss regularly:

Yearly priorities. At the beginning of each year, we identify five goals for the year, asking the question "What are the essential steps we need to take this year to thrive as a family?" (Here are some examples: make critical home repairs, improve our health and fitness, effectively manage the transition to the teen years, develop new shared spiritual practices.) Each time we meet for our family meeting, we review the progress we've made toward achieving these top-level goals.

Calendar and schedule. We look at our schedules for the upcoming week and coordinate activities that impact other family members. We also use this space to look further ahead and talk about when we may go on vacation or schedule doctor visits or a major home repair. As our kids got older, we started maintaining online calendars that we shared with one another so we could more easily coordinate our schedules.

Couple relationship. We spend some time checking in on our relationship, asking questions like "Are there any issues or tensions that we need to work through?" and "Is there any way we can better attend to and support one another?"

Personal growth goals. Each of us has personal growth challenges that we've identified and are committed to working on. We want to support one another in this process, so we take some time to listen, encourage and celebrate each other's progress. (We'll say more about this in chapter 6.)

Parenting decisions. Every stage in a child's life brings up new parenting challenges. So we take time to talk through our concerns and discuss how best to guide and interact with our children. This is also when we field emerging questions like "How are we going to navigate the use of media devices in our house?" or "What's our policy about riding in cars with friends?" and "What do we want to teach our kids about sex?"

Finances. Together we look at our family budget and talk about any upcoming financial decisions, including major purchases. Once a quarter we look at our spending records to see if we're keeping to our budget and note any adjustments that need to be made. Near the beginning of each new year, we review our spending patterns, anticipate upcoming expenses and create an annual spending plan.

Chores and household tasks. We talk through the details of how we keep house together and decide who will be responsible for various household tasks. We also discuss kids' chores and what our expectations and goals are for them as they gain homemaking skills and competencies. We also review our running prioritized list of household and home maintenance tasks, like tax preparation, home repairs, vehicle maintenance and remodeling projects. Even when we can't immediately attend to these tasks, it helps to know what's on our shared list so we don't feel like we need to bring them up at other times.

Soul care and other concerns. We talk about how we want to nurture one another spiritually and the ways we want to serve our neighbors. We also discuss any changes we may want to make in our ethics, shared habits or purchasing practices.

You could easily spend a whole day talking through these family life details. We usually set aside one to two hours for our family meeting. In the meeting, we briefly review each topic and then pick one or two to dive into. We keep minutes of our meetings so we have a record of what we discussed and decided.

Ideally, we have a family meeting every week. This doesn't always happen, but we find that when we meet consistently, life runs more smoothly, we get along better, and we feel more empowered to stay on track with our rhythms, goals and priorities.

Some people may find this strategy overly formal and businesslike. But in many ways, a family is like a business; it has an economy, team relationships, shared physical space and common tasks and goals. Your family is as important as any professional venture and deserves an equal amount of intentionality, communication and teamwork.

Whether or not this particular method appeals to you, every family needs some venue for planning and coordinating their shared purpose. If you don't have a strategy in place that works, try our family meeting method and then tweak it to fit your needs.

If you're parenting solo, you can set aside an hour or two a week for planning and decision making—and perhaps meet occasionally with a trusted friend or mentor who can be a sounding board and support your efforts.

If you are amicably coparenting with a former partner, it can be helpful to meet monthly or quarterly to talk about mutual decisions that affect your child's well-being. In some cases, it may be necessary to involve a third-party mediator to help coparents communicate and build consensus about shared decisions.

MAKING TRADEOFFS

When Amanda and Luke, introduced in chapter 1, created their family purpose agreement, they had a startling realization. Luke says, "With our work and travel schedules, we didn't have time to be the kind of family we wanted to be." They did the math and discovered that after paying childcare and transportation costs, they were benefiting only a few hundred dollars a month with both of them working full time. "When we saw the numbers, we looked at each other and thought, *What are we doing? Why are we working so hard and spending so many hours apart for so little?*"

Their answer had to do with inherited scripts and tradeoffs. Amanda grew up in a family of great wealth, and her mom didn't work. "I didn't want to end up like my mom," Amanda says. "She spent all her time watching television or socializing at the country club." Amanda hated to think that she was missing out on her children's early years simply because she didn't want to be like her mom.

Luke adds, "We didn't even consider the alternative that would be better for our family."

Eventually they decided that having both of them work full time was no longer worth what they got in return. Amanda resigned her position to search for part-time work in her field so she could spend more time with the people she loves the most.

The number-one complaint we hear from families is that they're stretched and busy. Busyness is the enemy of family thriving. Why are we so busy? In 1928, economist John Maynard Keynes predicted that the twenty-first-century standard of living would be so improved that no one would need to work more than three hours a day. His prediction didn't account for the fact that even when we have enough, we find more to want and do. We keep trying to cram more activities into our already full lives.

Our typical pace of life and rate of consumption are out of sync with the natural rhythms of our bodies and of the planet itself. As a result, the average American is highly stressed and financially leveraged—and the earth stands at the brink of ecological devastation.

The wise teacher of Ecclesiastes once said, "There is a time for everything." We can dare to believe that there are enough resources and time in our lives for everything that's essential. We can choose to approach the challenge of time with enthusiasm. Life is a gift and a sacred trust. You can find a pace of life in your family that has a satisfying rhythm, not too fast or too slow but just the right cadence to dance together in harmony with the divine order.

Looking at the disconnects between your family purpose and your current time commitments may leave you feeling deflated and discouraged. Maybe you're beginning to realize that you can't just add life-giving rhythms to an already full schedule. There are only twenty-four hours in a day and 168 hours in a week. To pursue what matters most, you have to make choices. "*Decide* sounds like *homicide*," Luke says, "because when you make choices, you're killing off other options."

Amanda adds, "And that was our problem: we didn't want to choose." Our choices make some things less possible and other things more possible.

How you spend your time is how you spend your life. And how you spend your life is shaped by choices with money. We each pay the price for the lives we've chosen. If you don't feel like you're getting to what is most important, it may be time to consider how you prioritize activities and make new tradeoffs. We all make choices and tradeoffs in the currencies of life: our time, money, relationships and possessions. If you want to own or consume more, you need to earn more, which will require more time working. Conversely, if you want more freedom and flexibility with your time, you may need to spend less energy working and maintaining possessions. Sometimes this is called an opportunity cost. Having more in one currency may cost in another. "Count the cost" is how Jesus described this wager (Lk 14:28).

Whatever we say yes or no to has a cost, and there are pros and cons to every decision. In our family, we chose meaningful but modest paying work and the freedom and flexibility to personally guide our children's education. The cost of these choices was living in a smaller space, having less disposable income and spending time and energy doing things for ourselves that we otherwise may have been able to afford to outsource.

Our chosen path also required significant emotional resources and internal motivation, which were costs we hadn't fully anticipated. Another family, by choice or necessity, may find the right rhythm in a different mix of decisions about time, money and material possessions. What's important is that these are considered and conscious choices.

You can find a mix of choices and tradeoffs that best supports your purpose as a family. Maybe your family needs more money to pay urgent bills, which will require more time working and less free time. Or you realize your family needs more time to connect, which will require less time working, commuting, doing separate activities or maintaining nonessential possessions.

Families often make new small or large changes that help them find a better life rhythm. Bethany and Jose loved the community work they got to do in their neighborhood. Both worked part time in local nonprofits, and together they homeschooled their two children. This arrangement worked for a long time, but at a certain point they were exhausted. It felt like they were working all the time, and money was still tight. What they needed was more emotional and financial sustainability. It took some time to adjust their expectations and ideals and to appreciate that one season of their life was coming to an end. Eventually they decided to send the kids to school and pursue work with better pay and benefits. This ultimately helped them gain more emotional stability and renewed energy to invest in their family.

Stephanie, Mike and their kids had what seemed like the American dream: a large house in a good neighborhood, private schools for the kids, great vacations and the promise of stock options and a healthy retirement. Mike's work as a corporate consultant took him all over the country. When he was in town, the days were full because of his long commute to the city. He had always reasoned that the quality of time spent with Stephanie and their kids made up for the lack of quantity. But Mike and Stephanie often had conflict in their marriage. When their youngest child started to struggle, they recognized it was time for a dramatic reboot. They decided to downsize their life. Mike found a job that required far less travel, but also paid less, which meant relocating to a smaller home and changing many of their spending habits.

We don't always have the option to reduce work hours, move or change jobs. But in these circumstances we can find small ways to move toward a more sustainable and life-giving rhythm. If you struggle to find contemplative time, pray while you're doing the dishes. Get some exercise by taking an early morning walk with the baby, who woke you up before sunrise.

Nicole is a single parent raising two children with special needs. She works full time to make ends meet and spends her evenings and weekends caring for her children and managing their education, diet and treatment plans. Life is full, and there isn't a lot that Nicole can do to change her situation. But she has found small ways to tweak her schedule. "I have childcare for an hour after I get off from work. So I try to spend thirty minutes alone, doing something relaxing before I go home." If she's diligent about getting the kids to bed on time, there's another space for chores or reflection. She saves a small amount each week so that once a year she can get a break and go on a trip by herself. "Finding those small pockets of time really makes a difference."

You decide what tradeoffs make sense for your family. Here are a few examples of tradeoffs families sometimes make to find a better rhythm for pursuing their shared purpose:

- Move closer to work or school to cut down on commute times.

- Downsize housing so less time has to be spent on cleaning, maintenance and yard work.

- Share housing or live close to a grandparent who can share life with your family.

- Choose to have one person do less work for pay so they can devote more time to family and household.

- Limit the number of activities family members participate in.

- Rethink expectations about what is necessary, and choose more simple, low-maintenance options where possible.

 REFLECTION: EXAMINING TRADEOFFS

Consider the tradeoffs you can make with your work, time, money and material possessions in order to pursue your family purpose and cultivate a sustainable rhythm. Discuss your responses to the following:

- Is there anything we've identified as important that currently doesn't have a designated slot in our schedule?

- What are the costs or tradeoffs of the decisions we've made? What has been made more possible or less possible because of these choices? Are we satisfied with the tradeoffs we're making?

- What are the life circumstances we've been handed that we can't change, and how can we better embrace and accept those limits?

- What do I want to communicate to my child about the choices and tradeoffs we've made?

- Are there any tradeoffs we need to make to have more time and energy for what's most important to us? Which of these changes are we ready to make right now?

 WHOLE FAMILY ACTIVITY

Choose one of the following activities to help your family cultivate healthy shared rhythms.

Establish or renew a family rhythm. If you've decided to establish a new family rhythm, take steps with your kids to enact it. Maybe you want to institute a family fun night or a new bedtime ritual. Having regular verbal reminders about what's coming next helps young children. "Okay, now we're going to have family story time."

As with so many things, your kids will be more on board if they are invited into the process. Take time to explain the new rhythm you're proposing and how you think it can help your family thrive. "We want to start having dinner together four nights a week so we can feel more connected," or "We'd like to have everyone stay in the kitchen after dinner and help until everything is cleaned up so that one person isn't left with the mess."

After sharing the proposal, ask if anyone has questions or concerns, and if they understand and agree to the change. This is an especially important step to take with older kids and teens who may be used to long-standing patterns or may need to adjust their expectations or schedule. Start your new rhythm, and after a week or two, talk about how it's going and if it's something worth continuing.

Set boundaries and limits on screen time. With the increasing prevalence of media devices and connectivity, it can be challenging for both adults and kids to discern how much time to spend in front of screens. It's easy to let screen time take up the space needed for important activities.

Many people find it helpful to have specific limits about when, where and how often they look at their devices. When our kids were small, we helped them monitor their screen time by introducing a token system, where each token represented thirty minutes. They could choose when to spend their tokens for screen time after schoolwork and chores. When the eight tokens in their jar were used up, their screen time for the week was done. With older kids and teens, you can have a conversation about the right amount of time in front of screens and come to agreements about and boundaries for how you engage with technology as a family. Here are some questions to discuss:

- Aside from school and work, what else do we do in front of screens? How does this time help and bring benefit to our lives?

- What is a good amount of time to spend each day or week on screen entertainment and social media?

- When we spend more time than this in front of screens, what are we missing out on in other areas of our lives?

- What are some boundaries and limits on screens that we can agree to that will help us thrive as a family (such as no screens during meals and family time, keep screen devices in a designated place overnight—away from bedrooms)?

Adjust the tempo. If you have teens, they're beginning to manage more of their time and schedule. You can help them develop skills to set a good rhythm for themselves, to prioritize what's important and to examine tradeoffs they may need to make. To begin, invite your teens to play you one of their favorite songs. Ask them to describe the elements of the music. What decisions did the artist make when writing this song? What is the beat like? What sonic elements are emphasized? Which sounds did the artist decide to leave out? Explain that life is like a song; certain elements are emphasized, and the parts find their balance. Then have a conversation about making good choices with time, including sharing from your own life experiences.

Here are some questions to ask:

- What is a healthy weekly schedule for you that keeps life in balance?
- What are the most important ways for you to spend your free time?
- What are your work and other commitments right now (school, chores, activities)?
- What relationships are important to you?
- What rhythms do we need in order to stay connected as a family?
- How are you engaging your passions?
- What do you need to do to take care of your body?
- What do you need to do to take care of your soul?
- When do you rest and play?
- Is there anything that needs to be added or eliminated from your schedule to have a better life rhythm?

RHYTHM, BY HAILEY JOY SCANDRETTE

I like to know what to expect and what's expected of me. I like getting new calendars, making to-do lists and reading course syllabi. Although I don't always come off as the most tidy or organized person (my room is usually cluttered, my sleep schedule is unpredictable), I love having expectations that I feel confident will be met.

When I was growing up, our weekly and daily family rhythms were a source of stability. I knew to expect to have dinner together unless other plans were made in advance. I knew that on Thursday nights we'd have Dad and Kid Night, while Mom went out and got a break. I knew that on Friday nights we'd all eat pizza and watch a movie and that on Sunday nights we'd check in as a family.

I could count on yearly traditions as well. I knew Mom would give us the day off of school for our birthdays, and we'd have breakfast in bed while we looked at baby pictures. I eagerly awaited the couple of weeks leading up to Christmas when we'd have Santa's Workshop days when we made gifts for friends and family.

Having an established rhythm built trust within our family. We were expected to show up for the rhythms of the day, the week or the year, and we expected Mom and Dad to do their part in upholding the sacredness of our traditions and routines. These rhythms provided space and time for checking in, for celebrating, for learning or playing together, and for supporting each other through rough seasons.

As we've gotten older, the rhythms have shifted to accommodate our changing needs. We still check in as a family once a week, ask each other about the highs and lows of the past seven days and pray for whatever challenges each person is facing. Sometimes the check-in is rushed by the necessity of homework or other outside commitments, but knowing that we'll all be in the same space soon, sharing about our lives, is comforting and valuable.

Rhythm is a powerful tool for ensuring that the way we choose to spend our time reflects what's most important to us. During the school year, my rhythms are mainly based on my schoolwork, my family, my friends and maintaining my emotional/spiritual landscape—all things that are important to me. Truth be told, I don't have this down yet. But due to our family practices, I have a solid framework for cultivating and striving for rhythms that will create space for the most important things in my life.

CHAPTER TASK CHECKLIST

- Identify your shared family rhythms.

- Reflect on tradeoffs.

- Engage in a whole family activity to explore shared rhythms. Try out a new family rhythm, set boundaries with screens, or explore priorities with your teen.

REVIEW OF KEY COMPETENCIES

Rooted. A thriving family enacts household rhythms and policies that are life giving and support the family's shared purpose.

- Our rhythm of life is sustainable with space for work, rest, play and meaningful celebrations.

- We have an effective venue and process for planning and decision making.

- We have agreements about how tasks will be accomplished.

- We're making conscious tradeoffs with our time and money to pursue what matters most.

- We're intentional about the amount of time we spend in front of screens and engaged with entertainment and social media.

4

A Thriving Family Discovers a Common Story

TWELVE PRIVATEERS STORMED CHINA BEACH, a cove nestled into a rocky cliff facing the Golden Gate Bridge. Enthusiastic about rumors of buried treasure, they searched among themselves for the map, only to find that it had gone missing. Avast! A pirate named Shifty Tom had stolen it. The crew of buccaneers found Shifty Tom and, by force of their swords, reclaimed the map. The map oriented them toward a rocky outcropping at the far end of the beach.

The sands had shifted in the waves, so they had to dig for what seemed like hours under the hot sun. Finally, one of their shovels struck a black wooden box. They hauled it up from the hole and pried it open to find a hoard of pirate booty: golden doubloons, skull-and-crossbones flags and sugar candy.

Cheering "Arr!" the pirates made their way to the galley, where the ship's cook had some grub laid out, complete with hard-tack biscuits and "rum." The ladies and gentlemen of fortune dove into their food, clanked their tankards and shouted, "Grr, happy birthday, Noah!"

This wasn't the first time, or the last, that a birthday party in our family included tricorn hats, crimson sashes and black eye patches. Pirate stories and true pirate history captured the imaginations of our kids for many years.

They loved stories of all kinds. *Goodnight Moon* soothed them with its familiar repetition when they were still small enough to cuddle on our laps. As they entered grade school, we read *The Chronicles of Narnia* while they sprawled on the living room floor, playing with LEGOs. The next day, during their play, they became Lucy, Peter, Edmund and Susan on an adventure with Aslan. They loved to be in this imagined world on a quest for what is true and good.

Contemporaries of Harry Potter, they understood his adolescent angst and the dilemmas he faced fighting against the forces of Voldemort. We also read Corrie ten Boom's account of her work with the Dutch resistance during the Nazi occupation and how she endured suffering in a concentration camp. We could see the faith and courage it took to do what was right in the face of substantial danger, and we had conversations about how we might hope to do the same. Reading aloud on long car trips, we met Huckleberry Finn, the Light Princess, Lizzy Bennet, the Glass family and many others.

All along we've read accounts from the Bible, looking for threads to connect its stories to ours. We've immersed ourselves in stories. To borrow from Dr. Seuss, we've read them "in a boat . . . with a goat . . . in the rain . . . in the dark . . . on a train . . . in a car . . . in a tree . . . they are so good, so good, you see!"

From cave paintings to video games, we are story-making and storytelling creatures. Stories help us know who we are and shape our imaginations as we explore and express what it means to be human. In stories, we observe the tension between good and evil. We see characters living boldly, doing challenging and courageous deeds, and rising above difficulties. Whether they are real or imagined, we want to be like the heroes who inspire us. What would Spiderman do? Storytelling plays a vital role in shaping moral imagination in a way that is far more effective than verbal discussions of abstract moral dilemmas.

What is the real story of the world? We naturally search for answers to the basic questions about our existence: Where was I before I was born? Why am I here? Who or what is God? And where do pets and people go when they die? Through thousands of years of religious history and practice, human beings have sought common understandings of our origins and destiny. In fact, the Latin root of the word *religion* means "to bind or connect." Having a shared understanding of a larger story helps us build trust, pursue common purposes and feel less alone in the universe. For this reason, family researchers often identify a shared religious core or concern for spiritual well-being as a key characteristic of healthy families.

Like pirates hunting for buried treasure, we search for a cohesive story that's true to life and can reliably guide us. *A thriving family cultivates awakening to God's care and the larger story we're all part of by embracing life-giving spiritual practices and making conscious ethical choices.* In this chapter, we'll explore how your family can cultivate receptivity and learn to live in God's larger story together.

EXPLORING GOD'S LARGER STORY

In his book *The Spiritual Lives of Children*, child psychiatrist Robert Cole documents children's thoughts about God and their experiences of the transcendent. One mother, Jessica, recalls the time when she "caught" her two-year-old daughter, Eleanor, singing a spontaneously created song to God as she rode along in her car seat.

Many of us can look back and remember moments of mystery in childhood: feeling an unseen presence while riding a bike, swinging back and forth on a swing, sitting in a church or being alone in nature. These common experiences beg the question posed by Teilhard de Chardin: Are we human beings that have spiritual experiences or spiritual beings having human experiences? The soul and the sacred are part of every aspect of our lives. In the words of Dallas Willard,

"We live in a God-bathed world." In childhood we experience divine reality and begin piecing together an understanding of God's larger story.

Many parents wonder if they're qualified to guide their child's understanding of God's story. You may feel pressure to impress exactly the right beliefs or practices on your kids. Or perhaps you hesitate to share much of anything because you don't want to say the wrong thing. Or you wrestle with your own doubts, questions or difficulties with belief. Isn't this a job best left to the professionals?

Talk to almost any children's minister or church youth worker, and they will tell you that parents have a much greater impact on faith formation than any weekly program they can offer. As a family, you have the tremendous opportunity to explore the most important questions of human existence together. Why is this such an important task for families? Because we live up to the stories we live under. Your understanding of the true story of the world significantly shapes how you belong to one another and who you are becoming together as a family. To say it another way, this is the *why* behind your family purpose agreement.

Of course, we aren't the first people who have gone on a search for the true story of the world. Thousands of years of human religion and civilization shape our mental categories and understanding, and we can learn from the knowledge, wisdom and experience of our spiritual ancestors.

When our daughter, Hailey, was three, we wanted to share our understanding of the Christian story with her. We used a colorful picture book that covered everything from the creation of the world to the afterlife and included vivid images of the golden streets of eternity as well as Jesus dying on the cross. Trying to be faithful to what we believed, we told Hailey, "Jesus wants you to be with him in heaven someday."

Her big, terrified eyes welled up with tears as she exclaimed, "I don't want to go with Jesus! I want to stay here with you, Mommy and Daddy!" Being taken away to an unfamiliar place by a bearded stranger in a robe didn't sound like good news to her. We put away the book, realizing that our sincere efforts had been misguided. Fortunately we had many other chances to explore God's story together.

Faith formation is a lifelong process, and parents as well as children keep growing in their experience and understanding of God's story. In his landmark research, developmental psychologist James Fowler identified six distinct stages of faith development throughout the lifespan. Young children engage faith primarily through concrete experiences, imagination, pictures and the people they relate to. School-age children often form a deep sense of universal justice and gravitate toward a literal understanding of Scripture. In adolescence, we develop the capacity for abstract thought, and this is often the time when people begin to own their faith for themselves and identify with a social group or institution that affirms their beliefs.

In early to middle adulthood, many people go through a period of angst and doubt as they critically examine their previous understandings, acknowledge inconsistencies and make comparisons with alternate views. A person in this stage may appear to be losing faith, but for many, this is a necessary step toward embracing mystery and paradox—a faith stage that's sometimes called the second naïveté.

We shouldn't be surprised by this natural and progressive process of faith development. As St. Paul observed, "We see through a glass, darkly." Throughout our lives, we continue to ask questions, checking to see if the version of the story we were told earlier is actually true to life. As Richard Rohr explains, when we're young, we need to "create a proper container" of concrete beliefs and moral structures. But eventually we may need to break the container to see things in a new way. The container of clear beliefs sets us on this necessary journey.

Technical details about faith stages may or may not interest you. What's important to understand is the likelihood that the people in your family are in various stages of faith formation and may have particular needs and sensitivities. As a parent, you may be in a place of doubt and reevaluation, while your children are at a stage when they may benefit from you helping them build concrete beliefs and a clear sense of right and wrong. Or you may really want your kids to know and affirm your faith tradition, but they aren't developmentally ready to process all the details or complexities you wish to share.

Faith formation fails when it spoon feeds answers to questions a person isn't even asking. We read stories for the pleasure of discovery. Hearing the conclusion too soon can spoil the journey. You can imagine how disappointed Noah and the other privateers would have been if they had been told to watch the adults dig up the treasure at his party. The satisfaction and fun is in the search and discovery.

Jesus once described the mystery of life with God as a treasure hidden in a field. The meaning of our lives is revealed in the process of the search. Here's how the book of Proverbs describes this journey,

> If you call out for insight
> and cry aloud for understanding,
> and if you look for it as for silver
> and search for it as for hidden treasure,
> then you will understand . . .
> and find the knowledge of God.

As a family, you can learn to explore the basic questions of human existence, God's story, in ways that are honest, truthful, compassionate and hopeful.

When our kids were first born, Mark read to them each day from the Psalms and Proverbs; it was a way that a busy parent could have some devotional time, and it helped the children learn to pay attention to his voice. During their toddler years, we used picture books to explore the great stories of the Bible together. Eventually we helped them memorize what we thought to be the most essential passages, using hand motions, songs and mnemonic devices to help them remember the words. These included the Lord's Prayer, the Ten Commandments, the Shema, the Golden Rule, Psalm 23 and Psalm 139.

When our kids were in early grade school, we began reading through the Bible together, usually a chapter or two a day around the dinner table with paper and crayons to keep little hands busy. The kids loved acting out many of the stories we discovered, especially David and Goliath, the nativity, Jesus calming the storm, the good Samaritan and the death and resurrection of Christ. Often Mark would ask some questions to get a discussion going about how that story relates to our lives and what we might do in response.

We tried our best to let the kids discover the Bible unfiltered, and our reading brought up all kinds of issues to discuss, like when the sons of Noah found him naked and drunk after he got off the ark. As the kids got into their teen years, we found it helpful to think carefully about how our faith relates to other faith traditions and contemporary questions in science, politics, literature, philosophy and current events.

We brought up questions, and the kids had questions of their own. How does the origins story in the book of Genesis relate to evidence of a very old planet and species evolution? Why did God tell the Israelites to kill people while Jesus teaches us to love our enemies? Hailey, in particular, wondered why there were so few female main characters in the stories of the Bible.

We haven't always had good answers to our kids' questions—and that's okay, because we're all on this story-exploring journey together. There's a clear difference between telling your kids what to believe and helping them learn to think carefully and critically so they can make informed choices. We can stay curious and invite them to lean into their questions while sharing what we believe to be true.

WHAT IS THE REAL STORY OF THE WORLD?

Because it's easy to get lost in the details of Scripture and the complexities of a faith tradition, we've found it helpful to keep in mind that the goal of this exploration is discovering how to live well in the real story of the world. As we read the ancient texts, we're looking for clues to help us understand our experiences of life—to form a cohesive narrative about who God is, who we are, why we are here and where this is all going. Whether you are deeply engaged in faith practices as a family or new to this kind of shared exploration, you can use the frame of a story to guide your search. Stories have basic themes that provide some handles for exploring the narrative arc of Scripture, history and contemporary life.

Every good story has a world. It could be the world of Gotham, ancient Greece, a galaxy far far away or the current world we inhabit. Here are some good questions to ask: What kind of world do we live in? Is it a good place to live? Where did this world come from, and who is in charge of it?

The Bible describes a world full of wonder and beauty, a world created by God that is "good." It's a world that reveals God's invisible qualities, eternal power and divine nature, understood from what has been made. It's a world where a loving, powerful and intelligent source is present and in charge. It's a safe place to be, where nothing can separate us from the eternal source of life and love. Here are some statements families have used to affirm this understanding of the real story of the world:

- Isn't this a beautiful world we live in?

- God brings us so many gifts to be grateful for!

- God is here with us, caring for us, helping us and guiding us.

- We have what we need.

- You don't need to be afraid.

- You are safe in God's world under God's care.

Every good story has compelling characters. We're captured by stories where the characters are interesting and relatable. Often the most popular character is the orphan or underdog who discovers their hidden worth and potential. Huckleberry Finn is one that is hard to forget.

Here are some good questions to ask: Who are the characters in the story of the real world? Who are we as human beings? What kind of creatures are we?

Genesis describes humans as powerful beings made in the divine image, the daughters and sons of the intelligence and love that spoke the world into existence. "Fearfully and wonderfully made," we possess great dignity, worth and responsibility. We can learn to find our truest identity as beloved sons and daughters of God. Here are some statements families have used to affirm this understanding of the real story of the world:

- You are fearfully and wonderfully made.

- We are each beloved sons and daughters of God.

- You are precious, important and valuable.

- God loves you.

- You are a powerful being, and you shape the world by your choices.

In the best stories, the characters are on a quest. They have an important task to accomplish. It may be finding love or a buried treasure or saving the world. They cause us to ask, Why are we here? What is the plot of the story we find ourselves in? And in the words of Wendell Berry, "What are people for?"

We were made for relationship with God, the One in whom "we live and move and have our being." We know and love God by learning to love and care for one another. As beings made in the image of the Creator, we shape the world by our words and actions. We rule, for better or worse, over ourselves and the rest of creation, making decisions that impact other creatures, the earth itself and future generations. We're on a quest to learn how to use our power and intelligence for good, as agents of wholeness and restoration, so that the kingdom of God becomes "on earth as it is in heaven." Here are some statements families have used to affirm this understanding of the real story of the world:

- You were made to know God's love and to share that love with others.

- You make choices, and those choices help or hurt.

- You can learn to use your power for good.

- We can say yes to God's reign and help heal the world.

- Our quest is to come to know and love God and to join God in bringing heaven and earth together again.

Every story presents a problem, conflict or challenge that must be overcome. Sometimes the struggle is monumental: dark forces are advancing; aliens threaten to destroy the planet. Sometimes the struggle is within: will the hero overcome their fear and summon the courage to make the right choice?

Looking at our lives and times we can ask, What is the human condition—the basic struggle of humanity? What threatens human flourishing? What obstacles keep us from the good and fulfilling lives we were created for? The intelligence, power and freedom we have allows us to choose whether or not to live under God's benevolent reign. We experience the natural consequences of our decisions. The choices we make lead us toward life and well-being or death and destruction. Though we were made for a life of flourishing under God's care, we have chosen to act from distorted thoughts about God, ourselves and one another, which Scripture calls sin. As a result, we've become alienated from God, from one another and from our true selves made in God's image.

We often act in ways that bring pain and brokenness to our world. Anger, jealousy, fear, worry, lust, greed and resentments are all signs of living in the dominion of darkness rather than in the light of God's care, reality and truth. Will we choose to acknowledge our missteps and return to the kingdom of love? Here are some statements families have used to affirm this understanding of the real story of the world:

- We don't always follow God's loving instructions to us, and this brings pain to others and us.

- We are beloved, but something inside of us is also very broken.

- We need the mercy and forgiveness that God offers each person.

- I see that you're feeling angry (or afraid, jealous, etc.). What do you want to do with those feelings?

- As you get older, your choices will become more and more powerful, so it's important that you practice choosing what is right and good now.

Epic stories reveal how the characters change and grow over time. Spoiler alert! Frodo learns to persevere and trust his friend until the ring of power is destroyed. Elizabeth Bennet overcomes her prejudices. Anakin Skywalker (a.k.a. Darth Vader) sacrifices himself to bring balance to the Force. We can ask, What is the path to awakening, enlightenment, salvation and eternal life? How can we recover the good lives we were created for?

God is continually inviting us to return to conscious awareness of our relationship with the divine and the truth of who we are. Jesus Christ is the clearest revelation of what God is like, and through his death and resurrection, he provides a path for living fully under God's loving reign. As a gift to us, God makes the way and invites us back onto the path; all we have to do is say yes. We learn to become all that we were made to be by following Christ's example and teachings. Here are some statements families have used to affirm this understanding of the real story of the world:

- To choose life, we need a source of love and power that is greater than our own.

- Jesus reveals what God is like; he makes and shows the way to become all that we were made to be.

- Is there any better example of what it looks like to love and be fully alive than Jesus? Many of the historical figures we admire most patterned their lives after his example and teachings.

- You can say yes to the free gift of life and surrender to the way of love.

 ## REFLECTION: EXPLORE YOUR OWN JOURNEY WITH GOD

You have the unique potential to explore God's larger story together as a family, inviting each other to say yes to life and to God's loving reign. Don't feel like you have to have all the answers before you begin. As an initiator, it may be helpful to spend time reflecting on your own spiritual journey, on how you have experienced God's care and presence in your life and on your current understanding of the larger questions of human existence. Use the questions below as journal prompts, and share your reflections with your spouse or a trusted friend.

First, reflect on your childhood faith formation.

- What are your earliest memories of divine mystery? When have you had experiences that you might interpret as God encounters?

- What have been the most significant moments and turning points in your experience and understanding of God and the larger story? Is there anything you wish had been explained differently when you were younger?

- Who are your heroes and the people you most admire? Why?

Now consider the basic elements of a story, and reflect on your understanding of the story of the real world.

- What kind of world do we live in? Is it a good place to live? Where did this world come from, and who is in charge of it?

- Who are we as human beings? What kind of creatures are we?

- Why are we here? What are people for? What is our quest?

- What is the human condition—the basic struggle of humanity? What threatens human flourishing? What obstacles keep us from the good and fulfilling lives we were created for?

- What is the path to awakening, enlightenment, salvation and eternal life? How can we recover the good lives we were created for?

CULTIVATING SPIRITUAL AWARENESS AT HOME

Rachel grew up in a family that was very involved in their church. In fact, her dad was a pastor, and both of her parents were well-known faith leaders. She remembers life as a kid revolving around public meetings and activities. Only as an adult did she begin to see it as strange that her family didn't pray or talk about God at home. "I knew my parents were very sincere and committed to their faith, but our family didn't have a shared spiritual awareness outside of church—and even at church we were usually in different rooms and programs!"

St. Paul reminds us that God doesn't live in buildings, yet we have the tendency to see certain times or places as more sacred than others or to emphasize the public expression of faith over the private. This is unfortunate, because where we need God's presence and guidance the most is in the midst of daily life and in our interactions with one another. Public faith gatherings can be a great support to families, but they aren't an adequate substitute for the life-on-life teaching and learning that can happen at home.

As parents, we have ultimate responsibility for guiding the spiritual formation of our children. Our homes have incredible potential to be a space where we intentionally encourage one another to be receptive to God and develop character, ethics and moral imagination. This resonates with the way faith formation happened in ancient Hebrew culture and still happens today in many observant households: "These commandments that I give you today are to be upon your hearts . . . talk about them when you sit at home and when you walk along the road, when you lie down and when you get up." In addition to taking advantage of the "teachable moments" that come up, like when your child comes home from school very upset, many families benefit from taking regular time together to acknowledge God's presence and reflect on the larger story together. Following are a few more examples of soul-shaping practices that many families have found helpful.

Talk about your own faith journey. Spend time telling your kids about the faith experiences that have shaped you, how your awareness of God developed and how your understanding has evolved over time. Speak about what you believe and why. With older children, don't hesitate to talk about where you struggle with belief. Sharing your faith journey with your kids can help them begin to reflect on their own path and experiences and to appreciate that faith formation is a lifelong process that their parents are still working out.

Shared learning. We've already mentioned several learning practices in this chapter, like reading and discussing Scripture and memorizing passages together. You might also read a book together, watch a film or news program, and have a conversation about the themes that come up and how they connect with God's larger story and the human condition. Get creative with how you engage and explore. Act out a story. Make up a song that helps you memorize a text. Paint a picture, build with LEGOs, or make a collage in response to what you've explored.

Prayer practices. Praying together is a powerful way to acknowledge God's care and presence. It can be as simple as offering a word of thanks at a meal. You could also use a psalm or written prayer from your tradition, write one of your own or sit together for a few moments in silence. Some families enjoy singing songs of thanks and adoration together. Tanya and her kids stop and pray whenever someone in their family gets hard news or is facing something difficult.

Faith community. Participation in a faith community can support and reinforce your family's desire to live in God's story together. And it can help you appreciate that you're part of a larger faith family. Faith community experiences can take many forms—from a liturgical church service to an intentional community that gathers in a home. It may also include service projects, youth programs, recovery and support groups, or a mix of several of these. What are the faith contexts that are meaningful for your family to connect with?

Rituals and traditions. The earliest followers of Jesus celebrated the Lord's Table as a meal in their homes to remember what Christ accomplished through his life, death and resurrection. Over time it has become more common to practice this sacrament in a public setting, but you may try doing it in the context of a family meal. We've found it meaningful to receive the elements around the dinner table by candlelight while looking one another in the eye and saying, "The body of Christ broken for you," and "The blood of Christ given for you."

Your holiday traditions can be another way to explore God's story together. During Christmas, focus on the gift of God's presence when the dark time of the year creates yearning for God's light and peace. Advent readings, songs by the tree, simple gifts and finding ways to serve neighbors can help you live with faith and hope in the renewal of all things. Easter proclaims the new life that's possible, and you can celebrate with reminders of the life that's bursting forth all around in spring.

We've also found a few minor holidays meaningful to observe. On March 17, we eat corned beef and cabbage, and we read St. Patrick's Shield and other Celtic prayers. On Martin Luther King Jr. Day, we remember the importance of the civil rights movement and read excerpts of sermons and speeches that inspire us to continue to work for justice and equality. For many years, on St. Valentine's Day, we prepared a dinner, complete with fancy dishes and dessert, and told our kids the story of our relationship. Much to their amusement, we even read excerpts from our old love letters.

Boundary crossings. In addition to your own faith community involvement, your family's understanding of God's story can be enriched by learning how faith is practiced among many different people groups. You may consider visiting churches in various traditions or faith gatherings of another ethnic or cultural group. When our kids were growing up, we had a chance to be part of Cambodian and Laotian churches. Many of our friends who are Jewish, Catholic or Buddhist have invited us into their celebrations that mark important milestones. In particular, we've found synagogue services and bar and bat mitzvah celebrations to be deeply moving. Engaging in various communities of faith can help you gain respect for a wide variety of cultures and traditions—and more fully appreciate and reflect on your own. You may be surprised by how much you have in common with others.

The practices we've mentioned in this chapter have been part of our toolkit for exploring the larger story together. Most were helpful for a season, and when the kids reached a new stage, we changed or adapted them to meet new needs and interests. Our goal was to do some kind of shared practice each day, but we didn't always succeed. This was fine, because what we were after was overall consistency, not slavishness to ritual. There are times when parents are tired, children are distracted and wiggly, or teenagers rolls their eyes at yet another conversation. That's okay; keep at it.

You can communicate, "This is our habit; it's what we do as a family. We connect, pray, read Scripture and talk about what matters most." Your spiritual engagement will not be magical every time, but consistency makes space and opportunity for moments of real connection to occur.

 WHOLE FAMILY ACTIVITY

You can develop a set of meaningful practices to help your family experience God's presence and live into the larger story together. First, decide on a regular time and place that works with your family's schedule and needs. You may want to start with five or ten minutes of focused activity at the table after a meal or before bedtime.

Read through the suggested list of tools below, and circle those that are a right fit for your family. If you have older gradeschoolers or teens, it may be helpful to ask which practices on the list sound most interesting to them and why. Then try out one or two of the practices you've identified this week. Parents and kids can take turns leading these readings, discussions or prayer activities. If this is a new or uncomfortable activity for you, don't feel like you have to do it perfectly; congratulate yourself for trying. Your efforts will add up over the months and years.

Sacred texts and stories.

- Read and discuss a passage of Scripture.

- Read a story or picture Bible.

- Draw or act out a story from Scripture.

- Memorize an important passage together.

- Read or watch a video about the life of a saint or historical figure you admire.

- Do a reading or liturgical practice from the seasons of the church calendar (Advent, Lent, Epiphany, etc.).

- Read stories from classic or contemporary literature that explore the larger themes of what it means to be human.

- Other: _____

Prayer and presence.

- Give thanks at mealtime.

- Share one thing you're grateful for today.

- Sing or listen to a sacred song together.

- Read or recite a psalm or written prayer.

- Pray about current needs and concerns.

- Sit for a few minutes in silence to remember the Maker's presence.

- Other: _____

Community practices.

- Participate together in a faith community.

- Celebrate holidays with friends and relatives.

- Share the story of your spiritual journey with your kids.

- Introduce a conversation about a new practice or project you'd like to do together that reflects your values.

- Other: _____

LIVING A GOOD STORY TOGETHER

Children are more likely to adopt the faith path of their parents if they believe that their parents live in the real world—that is, if they see Mom or Dad living out belief with honesty and practicality. As parents, we can model and pursue an authentic spiritual path that works in the real world. How we live is as important as what we say we believe. Or to say it more accurately, we show what we actually believe is true by how we live our lives.

Jesus once said, "Everyone who hears these words of mine and puts them into practice is ... wise." As a family, you have the incredible opportunity to live into the real story of the world together. What new steps can you take to live out the teachings of Jesus and the good instructions of Scripture together? You can initiate taking steps to respond to the truth and wisdom you've explored. Here are a few examples:

- Jesus told a story about a feast where everyone was invited, including outsiders and the most unlikely people. Is there anyone like this in our town or neighborhood? Who do we know who is lonely? When could we invite them to feast with us?

- Dr. Martin Luther King Jr. and others involved in the civil rights movement of the 1960s were motivated by deep faith and conviction. They worked for practical changes in laws and policies that were unfair and unjust. What are the current struggles for justice in our time? How can we be involved?

- Our friend Joe just got out of the hospital and needs a place to stay for a few days. How would you feel about inviting him to stay with us? In his condition, he'll probably need a private place to sleep. Would you be willing to give up your room for the week so we can show Joe care and hospitality?

In our family, we like to try shared experiments, where we take steps to live out the teachings of Jesus and the Scriptures together. Sometimes our experiments start with the Gospels, and other times our practice develops in response to a current crisis or news story. We want what we discover to impact how we live, and we want to support each other in making changes.

When our kids were in grade school, we read *Chew On This* by Eric Schlosser, the children's version of his book *Fast Food Nation*, about how the fast-food industry affects health, restaurant and farm workers, animals and the land. The kids, along with us, were really stirred by what we discovered. We had a conversation about how to change our eating and purchasing habits. We also referenced Isaiah 58, a prophetic text about how caring for workers, orphans, widows and the poor is part of loving God.

Together we decided that there were certain restaurants where we would no longer eat until they changed their practices. We also talked about what this choice would cost us. It would mean, for instance, that when we went on road trips, instead of stopping for burgers and fries at a fast-food restaurant, we would need to pack a picnic ahead of time. The kids were very supportive of making this change, because they understood why we were doing it and were involved in the decision making.

 ## FAMILY MEETING: INVITE ONE ANOTHER INTO COMMON ACTION

As a family, you can invite each other to take steps to put the wisdom of God's story into practice. Wise parents don't just tell their kids what they want to change or do, they involve the whole family in the process. This can start with one or two family members proposing a shared action or practice—anything from changing your media habits to volunteering at a soup kitchen, or a big change like adopting a new family member. Think of a new step you would like your family to consider taking, and share your process with your spouse. Later you can initiate a conversation with the whole family to see if they're ready to take this step together. In your notebook, record the following:

- What I would like us to do or change
- The reason(s) I'm proposing this action and how this relates to God's larger story
- What it may require of each person in our family

DOWN-TO-EARTH SPIRITUALITY

When our kids were young, we discovered the legacy of a fifth-century teenager named Patrick, who was snatched from his home by pirates and taken as a slave to Ireland. Years after his escape, he returned to Ireland from Britain to establish what has become known as Celtic Christianity, which is distinguished by its rootedness in earth cycles and the mysteries of nature. Celtic prayers were often written about everyday activities, such as fetching water, breastfeeding and walking out the door to begin a journey.

As a family, we began to wonder what it would look like for us to create prayers that express awareness of God in everyday tasks. At that time, our son Isaiah was potty training. He had accomplished urinating in the toilet but was struggling to master number two. We thought this might be a great opportunity to create a Celtic-style prayer. So Mark wrote a "poopy prayer" for Isaiah that we said together at mealtimes:

Jesus, hear my poopy prayer.
No more poopies in my underwear!
When I feel it in my body,
help me put it in the potty.

The prayer was fun to say and made Isaiah laugh hysterically. And believe it or not, within three days he had mastered the art of putting his poopy in the potty.

At its best, shared understanding of a larger story isn't just about ancient texts or rituals. It's a living story, the real story of our world that we participate in together.

STORY, BY HAILEY JOY SCANDRETTE

I'm a sucker for a good story. Actually, *sucker* doesn't quite capture it. I use stories to make sense of life: made-up stories, factual stories and stories that are utterly true without having actually happened.

I'm convinced that storytelling is one of the key things that makes us human and allows us to create a shared humanity. This means stories are incredibly powerful.

The stories we tell ourselves shape how we interact with the world and how we approach the challenges and opportunities in our lives. We all tell ourselves both true and false stories about our place in the world. Learning to differentiate between the true and false narratives enables us to engage God and find our true selves. Having false narratives is part of being human. We struggle with anxiety, fear, envy, perfectionism, anger, etc., because these are human responses to the uncertainty of being alive. However, when these responses go unchecked, they become part of a story we tell ourselves that keeps us from growing and living more fully in the kingdom of God.

It's a lot of work to change the narrative you tell yourself. It takes effort just to identify what that narrative is. Growing up, we were taught to start this process by understanding the biggest, truest things about our story. We were given the opportunities from a very young age to process and discuss the larger story of God and Jesus as told in the Bible. As a family, we read Scripture together at least three or four times a week. We were encouraged to ask questions and to share our interpretation of the message being communicated.

Our parents attempted to present us with what they believed to be the most important truths about the story of God's relationship with humans: that we're deeply and unconditionally loved, that Jesus shows a better way of being, that we're called to love others unconditionally as we're loved, etc. They also encouraged us to discuss these truths and the passages that contain them, which gave us ownership of our personal beliefs and allowed us to build an ever-growing concept of our independent spirituality.

As an adult, I don't think I fully understand how grounding it has been to find myself in the larger context of the grand story of God's relationship with humanity. It gives me a sort of baseline context for who I am and provides a reference for understanding when I'm struggling with a false narrative. It's helpful to confront those false narratives by asking, "How is this way of thinking preventing me from living into the larger, truer story?"

CHAPTER TASK CHECKLIST

- Reflect on your own spiritual journey and what you want to share with your kids about your understanding of God's larger story.

- Choose a spiritual practice to try as a whole family activity.

- Talk about a new step you want to take to put your values and beliefs into practice.

REVIEW OF KEY COMPETENCIES

Receptive. A thriving family cultivates awakening to God's care and the larger story we are all part of by embracing life-giving spiritual practices and making conscious ethical choices.

- We explore and articulate our understanding of the larger story in open dialogue.

- We have shared life-giving spiritual practices that help ground and sustain us.

- We have a venue to sharpen our thinking and discuss values, ethics, beliefs and the important needs and opportunities in our world today.

- We make shared choices about how to deepen the practice of our ethics and values.

- To the best of our ability, we're living out our deepest values with consistency, and we're honest when we aren't.

A Thriving Family Fosters Connection

WE OWN A LITTLE CAR that looks like a toaster on wheels. Bought when our kids were in grade school, its compact size makes it easy to fit into parallel parking spaces, and it gets great gas mileage. It's an ideal vehicle for an urban family. Now that the kids are full size, packing into our car, especially for an overnight trip, is like a game of Tetris. We parents are both above average in height, but we look tiny compared to our sons, who are broad shouldered and well over six feet tall. It takes a lot of patience and communication just to get seated and buckled. The only way we fit is if our tallest son, Noah, rides shotgun, and one of us sits in the middle of the back seat. When we unload at our destination, people stare in amazement as if we're performing a circus trick.

Even though our kids are now young adults, one of the traditions they insist we maintain is Christmas tree cutting on Thanksgiving weekend. We pack a picnic, fold ourselves into the little toaster and drive down the coast to Rancho Siempre Verde Tree Farm. Since we now walk or bike most places, and the kids take the subway to the university, it's rare to be in the car all together. And doing so brings back a flood of memories.

On longer trips when the kids were younger, they would get restless, and someone would inevitably exclaim, "Stop leaning on me!" or "Keep your feet away from mine!" To distract them and pass the time, Mark would read a book out loud, tell a story or teach the kids a sacred or silly song.

As we roll down the road toward the tree farm, Isaiah starts singing some of the silly songs Mark taught them years ago—"The Song That Never Ends," "My Name Is Jan Johnson" and another favorite about Comet, vomit and Listerine—and we all join in. In the pause after our voices are hoarse, Hailey says, "Remember that time Dad had us roll down the windows and cheer, 'Our mother is a lactational diva! Our mother is a superstar!'"

Lisa chips in. "Well, the first part wouldn't be true anymore."

But for old time's sake, and to Lisa's chagrin, we roll down the windows and chant, "Our mother is a superstar! Our mother is a superstar!"

At the tree farm, Lisa lays out a picnic, and we roast sausages and marshmallows over an open fire. The boys are eager to carve roasting sticks and grill up a sausage for the superstar. After lunch, we start the search for the perfect Christmas tree, and as is our custom, we have a playful debate about which tree to choose. Then we take turns suggesting the most improbable, stubby, crooked or ginormous tree that stands before us. At this point, one of us says something funny and a bit off-color, which becomes the inside joke we repeat and expand the rest of the day.

After Isaiah ceremoniously cuts the tree, we snap pictures and then haul it to the little toaster and tie it onto the roof. On the way home, we stop at a lighthouse for a short stroll and snap more pictures during the golden hour. As we continue up the coast, the sun sets, and our mood shifts from laughter to a silence that befits the fading light of dusk. Noah turns on the radio, and we listen to a lecture on climate change that gets us talking passionately about the aches and challenges in our world.

Not every Christmas tree day has felt as idyllic as this one. There were times when sickness, teenage hormones or other pressures dampened the mood and our harmony. And yet we're grateful that, after all these years, we can still have so much fun and feel so connected.

Feeling connected and having fun together is the fuel that propels a family forward into its shared purpose. We need to belong before we can become. A warm, positive home is both a gift of grace and an intentional practice. *A thriving family relates with love and respect and pursues healthy ways to connect, communicate, navigate conflicts and have fun.* In this chapter, we'll explore skills and practices that can help the members of your family feel safe, supported, connected and loved.

CREATING A POSITIVE FAMILY CULTURE

We all want to be part of family systems that are healthy, supportive and connected, but family cohesion is still so rare that when we see it, we take note. "Wow, they are so close, and they love each other so much!" The ancient psalmist praised this kind of connectedness:

> How very good and pleasant it is
> when kindred live together in unity!
> It is like the precious oil . . . ,
> running down upon the beard
> on the beard of Aaron.

Family unity doesn't happen by accident; it takes effort and teamwork. Think for a moment about your favorite sports team. To be a championship team, the players need to have excellent skills, but more importantly, they must play well together. Good coaching makes all the difference. Effective coaches cast a vision, set expectations, manage player relationships and keep team morale up. In your family, you are a team captain, you play on the team, and you are responsible for helping the team play well together. A family isn't just a collection of individuals but a dynamic system of relationships, and that's why your leadership is crucial. Being a player and a coach at the same time is hard work, but it often makes the difference between a family that simply coexists and one that's supportive, close and moving toward a shared purpose.

In your family, you have the opportunity to cast a vision and set expectations about how you will treat one another. You may think of this as the set of ground rules or as the constitution that guides how you relate to one another. One rule that Pete and Jackie, parents of two toddlers, try to communicate to their kids is "We treat each other with love and respect, based on the Golden Rule: 'Do to others as you would have them do to you.'"

When our kids were small, we used hand and body movements to help them learn what Jesus called the two greatest commandments: "Love the Lord your God with all your heart and with all your soul and with all your strength and with all your mind"; and, "Love your neighbor as yourself." We called these our yes commands and explained that love requires us to say yes to some actions and no to others.

Over time we asked the kids, "How should we treat each other? What do we need to say yes and no to in order to love each other?" The kids came up with a list that looked something like this:

- Speak kindly (don't yell or call each other names).

- Tell the truth (don't lie).

- Listen to Mom and Dad.

- Respect people's bodies (don't hurt them or touch without permission).

- Respect people's belongings (don't take their toys or food).

This had a striking resemblance to many of the Ten Commandments: Honor your father and your mother, do not kill, do not steal, do not lie. Eventually we taught them the commandments using hand motions, though several of them required simpler language. "You shall not commit adultery," for instance, became "Only share your body with the person you're married to." And "you shall not covet" became "do not want what belongs to your neighbor."

Whenever possible, we tried to state our ground rules in the positive—our "yes rules," we called them. There were also some "no rules" that we realized we needed only when they were violated. "We don't hit each other" was a rule we found necessary to articulate when our kids started using their fists to solve their problems. We had to pause and remind them of our culture of love and respect: "Look at these hands. These hands were made for helping, not for hurting."

We found it important to explore how our rules help us have good relationships with one another—for example, "We have a rule about telling the truth, because when we lie, it makes the people in our lives less likely to trust us. Think of how it would affect our relationships if we didn't trust one another." When we understand the logic—the "why"—behind a rule, we're more likely to embrace it from a place of deep internal agreement.

 ## WHOLE FAMILY ACTIVITY

Here are some activities that can help you cultivate a culture of love and respect. Choose one that best fits your family situation right now, and try it.

Explore your ground rules. Though you likely have some family ground rules in place, it can help to revisit those rules and the logic behind them at different stages of family life. Involving your kids in the process will give them greater ownership; we are all more likely to support rules that we help create and articulate. Here are some questions to guide your discussion:

• How do we want to treat each other? What are the rules that will help us have the kind of relationships and family culture we want?

- What behaviors do we need to say yes to and what do we need to say no to in order to treat each other with love and respect?

- Is there a passage of Scripture that provides a meaningful expression of our family culture of love and respect?

- What might help us remember how we want to treat one another?

Cheer each other on. As a coach, you can take steps to keep morale up and remind other family members that you are all in this together. Jarrod and Taryn chant their son's name: "Benton! Benton! Benton!" Other friends, Jeanne and Jarrett, even have a hashtag for their family cheer: #weareteamstevens. Before entering a new or uncomfortable situation, our family might huddle up, pray, put our hands together and shout, "Go, team, go!"

Giving hugs and regularly saying, "I love you" is a great way to help family members feel safe, cared for and loved. Calling each other by nicknames is a lighthearted way that many families express affection and closeness—if family members want to be called by their nicknames. Our kids like to call Mark Pops or Papa, and Mark has many pet names for the rest of the family, including Champ, Bubba, Spanky and Baby Mama (and Superstar).

Speak affirmations. Amid the pressures and demands of life, encouraging words can bring energy and hope. Many families find it helpful to create intentional spaces to appreciate and affirm one another. In our family, this happens every few weeks around the dinner table, or whenever we think people could use a little extra cheerleading. An affirmation is a statement that expresses delight in the specific qualities of a person. Here are a few examples:

- "You make me laugh. I like spending time with you."

- "I love watching you get so excited about what you're learning. You are a really passionate person."

- "I see that you care deeply about your friends. You are a good friend."
- "You have a lot of integrity—living out what you believe."
- "Thanks for making me food. You are a good cook."

This week, gather your family and take turns affirming one another. Pick someone to start with, and invite each family member to offer an affirmation to that person. What is something you like about this person? How do they bring good to your family and our world? It's important that each person has something to share, and it's okay if multiple people share similar affirmations. After each person has shared, move on to the next person.

Some family members may find it easier than others to think of affirmations on the spot, so be patient and encouraging. Others may find it slightly uncomfortable to be in the spotlight, receiving praise. Whatever the challenges may be, this can be a very powerful way to cultivate a culture of care and support, and it's something we get better at with practice.

Share highs and lows. St. Paul wrote, "Rejoice with those who rejoice; mourn with those who mourn." You can create a culture of warmth by celebrating good news together and supporting each other through difficulties. A simple and practical way to do this is by sharing your highs and lows of the day or week. Each person takes a turn telling about one good thing and one hard thing. This often provides a good opportunity to pray for each other and teach coping strategies.

Sometimes a child will need extra help finding words for what they are feeling. "You seem really sad. Can you tell us what you're feeling?" Children may also need help identifying exactly why they're upset. Doing this together regularly will help family members develop empathy and caring skills that they can take into other relationships.

Initiate a family check-in to keep short accounts. "Live in harmony with one another." Sharing so much of life in the same space almost inevitably leads to rubs and slights between family members that can negatively impact the mood and unity of a household. When you sense tension building, gather people together to do a quick check-in to make sure everyone is at peace with each other. You can introduce this by saying something like "We want to live in harmony with one another, but we occasionally do or say things that hurt each other. Sometimes we don't even know the hurt we've caused. Let's take a few minutes to check in and make sure we're at peace. Is there anyone at the table that you have hurt that you would like to make things right with? Is there anyone at the table that you feel hurt by?"

Have some fun together. In family life, there's a lot of hard and serious work to do. That's why having some serious fun together is so important. Fun times are like the grease that keeps relationships running smoothly when the demands of life heat up. Play a silly game. Try out a new food. Eat ice cream for dinner on a hot summer night. Have a family night where each person gets to choose a favorite activity for everyone to do together for twenty or thirty minutes.

MAKING REPAIRS IN RELATIONSHIPS

We had been looking forward to our vacation in Palm Springs for months—with visions of hikes in Joshua Tree, fun times around the swimming pool and afternoons watching dollar matinees in an air-conditioned theater. Mark made reservations at a vintage tiki motel where Elvis once swam in the pool. And Lisa shopped for our favorite picnic foods and snacks.

As we drove the eight hours from our house to Palm Springs, we listened to a road-trip playlist we'd made that included our favorite songs by the Beach Boys, the Beatles and Johnny Cash, with a few tracks from U2's *Joshua Tree* thrown in for good measure.

The room was spacious. The pool was radiant. The weather was perfect. Conditions were optimal for a fun and relaxing week together. We even kicked off the first night with a pizza party out by the pool under the tiki torches. But it didn't take long for the kids to start squabbling about who got to use the snorkeling mask, who had to share a bed and who got to pick the next cartoon to watch. We parents weren't any better, snapping at the kids to stop bickering and taking out our fatigue and frustrations on each other.

On the third night, we had what we've come to call a family vacation meltdown, complete with hot tears and angry words, followed by several hours sitting on hotel beds, trying to make repairs. As it turned out, we had packed some unplanned luggage that had the potential to wreck our vacation—ourselves.

The members of our family are our very favorite people. We love each other deeply. So why is it that sometimes we find it so difficult to show up for one another in kind and loving ways? What our vacation story illustrates is that connecting as a family requires more than simply being together. We're broken people in need of growth. In close contact, our brokenness rubs together and begins to reverberate, resulting in unpleasantness, avoidance and conflict. We are each on the journey to becoming more whole and better formed as people—fully present and living from the center.

Looking back, we can see how inner disorder and unmet needs contributed to our vacation meltdown. As parents, we had spent several days rushing to get ready for our trip. In the absence of distractions, the depth of our fatigue was catching up with us. Everyone in our family struggled, to some extent, with distorted scripts like these:

- "I can only be happy if I get what I want."
- "Nobody in this family cares about my needs."
- "I work so hard, and no one seems to respect or appreciate what I do."
- "I just need to be alone!"

In our house, things get broken. We don't always treat each other with the love and respect we each deserve. We get angry. We say hurtful words. We fail to communicate. We don't follow through on our commitments. When family ground rules are broken, it can cause ruptures in relationships. When this happens, families can take steps to make repairs by admitting mistakes, seeking forgiveness and building greater understanding.

Finding constructive ways to deal with conflict is one of the essential skills a family can develop. The intimacy of family life makes it especially important to keep short accounts. In casual relationships, if one person hurts another, you could simply choose to withdraw. But in a shared household, making repairs is crucial if there is to be warmth, safety and trust among family members. Neglecting those repairs over time can result in distance, deep wounds and resentments between marriage partners, between children and between children and parents.

The teachings of Jesus offer realistic and practical wisdom for dealing with the ruptures that can happen between family members:

- Seek reconciliation with those you have hurt.

- When someone wrongs you, speak to that person directly.

- Relentlessly forgive one another.

We're all on the journey of learning how to keep short accounts, forgive one another and express our needs and desires in constructive ways. From a neurological perspective, making repairs in relationships actually strengthens the bonds of intimacy between two people. A good fight that helps you work through conflict, rather than avoiding it, will strengthen intimacy and trust. Kelley, parent to two adopted children, describes what this looks like in her family:

> My son and I sometimes provoke one another. One night, while quite upset, he blurted out, "I know you regret adopting me!" I took a deep breath. Then I told him that I've never regretted adopting him, but that my frustration often comes from my own

insecurity as a mother—am I a good enough mother for you? This moment of vulnerability opened a door for us. He saw my humanity, my own struggle to become a better mother. We are learning together that it is hard to grow up and hard to raise up a child! We have a three-point apology in our house which includes saying what we did to offend or hurt the other person, saying we are sorry while looking in their eyes and suggesting how we can "make it right." We believe this final step pushes us to practice restitution—to suggest actions like "I will do your chores for a day" or "I will give you my toy to replace the one I broke." When we don't know what making it right may look like, we ask the other person. Sometimes it is as simple as offering a hug!

Many families find it helpful to have an agreed-upon process and clear steps for working through conflict and making repairs. Here's a template of steps we've found helpful:

Step 1. Stop and talk. A good fight starts with one of us recognizing that a rupture has occurred and then initiating a check-in, saying something like "Hey, can we talk? I'm feeling some tension." We agree on a time and place to talk, preferably as soon as possible. It's difficult to think or talk clearly if our emotions are in a heightened state, so we take five or ten minutes to calm down before starting our conversation. When possible, we try to talk in private, although one couple we know says their best arguments take place in public spaces, "perhaps because we are more kind and generous when there are others around."

Step 2. Listen to each other. We've found it extremely helpful to have established ground rules for how we communicate during conflicts, because the posture and tone of our responses can either magnify tensions or encourage resolution. Here are the ground rules we try to use in our family:

- *We seek to listen and understand the other person's perspective*, assuming the very best about their motives and intentions. The person we are in conflict with is someone we deeply love who is on the same team.

- *We use "I" statements and avoid accusations or universalizing words like "always" and "never."* Instead of saying, "You *always* leave the kitchen a mess because you don't value what I do," it's far more constructive to use "I" statements and stick with the facts: "You left the kitchen a mess this morning. When you do this I feel like my time and effort aren't being valued."

- *We're committed to staying engaged until the issue is resolved.* No one leaves the room without permission. If we need a bit of space to calm down, we make a request to leave while affirming our commitment to stay in the process.

- *We focus on how the other person's words or actions affected us* rather than making judgments about their motives or character. Instead of saying, "You don't respect me, and you don't even care that you embarrassed me in front of our guests," a better and more accurate response would be "When you spoke sharply to me in front of our guests, I felt embarrassed and disrespected."

- *We seek to deal with the current situation* without bringing up past wounds or offenses that have already been addressed and resolved.

- *We speak to each other in a normal tone of voice,* avoiding yelling and profanity.

Any of us can remind the other person of our ground rules at any point in the conversation and request that those rules be abided by. "The way you just spoke to me is not how we agreed to communicate. Please try again and say it a different way." If we're finding it especially difficult to maintain composure, we find it helpful to carry out our conversation in written form by passing a notebook back and forth.

Step 3. Own your part. Conflict is rarely one-sided. Usually each person feels wronged or misunderstood in some way. So restoring harmony often involves each person owning what they can, asking for forgiveness and taking practical steps to correct the situation. This requires more than just saying, "I'm sorry." A fuller apology communicates "Here's what I did wrong. I'm sorry I hurt you. Will you forgive me? What can I do to make things right?" We've found that we can resolve tensions much more quickly if each person feels heard and is willing to acknowledge their part in the conflict. Here are a couple of statements that express ownership and responsibility.

- "I know I left the kitchen a mess, and I'm sorry. I was late for a meeting and needed to get out the door quickly. As a rule, I do think I should be cleaning up after myself. I do value your time and appreciate your patience. I notice you already cleaned up my mess. Can I offer to clean up the kitchen after dinner this evening?"

- "I didn't mean to speak sharply. I'm sorry it came out that way and can see why you felt disrespected. Will you forgive me? Next time we're with friends, I'm going to be extra careful to speak to you respectfully."

Step 4. Give and receive forgiveness. When we have each had time to seek understanding, communicate our perspective and own what we can, we try to ask for and express forgiveness, letting each other know that there's no longer a rupture between us. Often one of us will ask, "So are we okay now?" And the other person might say, "It helps me to know that you didn't intend to leave your mess. I forgive you. Thanks for hearing me out. I'm sorry I took this so personally."

Step 5. Affirm love. After a conflict, we offer kisses or hugs and kind words to bring closure and affirm our love for one another. Research suggests that we remember negative comments and events far more clearly than we do positive ones. To offset each negative interaction, we need to have five positive ones. Those positive affirmations are like savings in our relational bank accounts; they keep conflicts from depleting our emotional reserves.

Step 6. Explore solutions. Sometimes a conflict stems from differing expectations, poor communication patterns or ineffective ways of getting things done. Conflict can signal the opportunity to establish clearer boundaries or a better household policy. After we've reconciled, we find it helpful to ask each other, "How can we arrange life differently so that this tension is less likely to arise in the future?"

Conflict can also be the alarm that alerts us to someone's need for extra care, space, prayer or support. A skill that has been extremely helpful in our family is learning to express our needs and desires to one another, trusting that if other family members know what we need, they will do what they can to support us. Sometimes we're able to anticipate potential ruptures and warn the family about our vulnerable state. Here's an example of what may be said: "Just so you know, I'm feeling very tired and emotional tonight, and I don't have the resources I normally do. I need you to be gentle with me. If there's something potentially difficult we need to discuss, let's schedule that conversation for another time."

When we're sad, sick, tired, stressed or discouraged, it's more challenging to treat each other with love and respect. We try to give each other an extra measure of grace in these situations. We don't excuse bad behavior, but knowing the underlying causes makes it easier to be compassionate and understanding.

FAMILY MEETING:
PRACTICE MAKING REPAIRS

It's easier to learn how to be assertive, make repairs and resolve conflicts when you aren't in the heat of the moment. If you tend to be conflict avoidant, practice can help you grow in the confidence that the process of dealing with relational tensions is worth the risk. During your next family meeting, take time to establish ground rules for communication. Then talk through a recent rupture or point of tension in your relationship. If you're parenting solo, practice doing this with a trusted relative or close friend.

- *Stop and talk.* What are the ground rules you both agree to follow when you're working through conflict?
- *Listen to each other.* What happened or what's not working? How does this make you feel?
- *Own your part.* What part of this conflict can you own? What would you like the other person to acknowledge?
- *Give and receive forgiveness.* What do you need to ask forgiveness for? What are you ready to forgive?
- *Affirm love.* What can you say right now to affirm your love and commitment to each other?
- *Explore solutions.* What can be done to correct the situation? Is this an opportunity to clarify better expectations or negotiate a new household policy?

 ## REFLECTION: EXPLORE WHAT TRIGGERS CONFLICT

Kyle and Hannah got into a fight while they were cleaning the house to prepare for a visit from Hannah's parents. Kyle pointed to a large pile of dirty clothes stacked in the corner of their bedroom and said, "Hannah, can I take these clothes to the laundry room to wash?"

The clothes were Hannah's, and she snapped back, "Why don't you just deal with your own stuff! Look at that dish and coffee cup on the dresser. You should stop bringing dishes into our bedroom."

Kyle looked at the dishes and then loudly exclaimed, "I brought those dishes in here this morning—but that huge pile of dirty clothes has been stacking up in the corner for weeks!"

"Kyle, keep your voice down," Hannah said. "You're scaring the kids."

That was the beginning of a long argument that played out in front of their children. Kyle was simply trying to help, but Hannah was feeling embarrassed by the pile of laundry, insecure about her home-making skills and anxious about her parent's visit. When she drew attention to his angry voice in front of the children, he felt deflated and defensive. Suddenly they were both in fight-or-flight mode, flooded with emotions. Reflecting later, Kyle said, "Our fights may start with clothes or dishes, but it's never just about the laundry."

Ideally we would all be quick to admit when we're wrong, slow to become angry and quick to forgive. But each of us finds certain aspects of navigating conflict challenging. Some of us tend to express our anger or disappointment explosively. Others of us may withdraw to avoid conflict, finding it difficult to bring up hurts or express needs, reasoning that it's less painful to suppress or ignore negative feelings.

Conflict arises when one or both people aren't feeling loved or respected or when deep wounds or insecurities are triggered. When we get triggered, we tend to "lose it" and react from raw emotion and sometimes irrational thoughts.

In addition to developing skills for constructive conflict, it can be helpful to examine the inner thoughts and feelings that shape your responses to relational tension. The way conflict was dealt with in your family of origin and any trauma you have experienced likely impact how you respond to disharmony. Conflict brings up our need for inner transformation. To be fully present to care for one another, we need a source of love that is greater than our own.

Consider the patterns in your conflicts with your spouse or other family members, and write a response to the following questions:

- What skills do you bring to the process of resolving conflict (such as initiating conversation, active listening, "I" statements, asking for forgiveness, offering forgiveness, making corrections)?

- Which of these skills do you find more difficult to practice?

- What triggers you or where do you feel particularly vulnerable in your relationships?

- What can you remember and affirm the next time you're triggered that will help keep you from losing it? What's the inner work you can do to tap into God's infinite love?

HELPING KIDS WORK THROUGH CONFLICT

In the urgency of the moment, while guiding or correcting a child, it's easy to speak harshly, make snap decisions or bring false accusations. In the face of an adult who is angry or behaving poorly, a child will often assume they are responsible for their parent's negative emotions—and internalize that unintended message. One of the most powerful things you can do as a parent is apologize to your child when you make a mistake, and ask for forgiveness.

In our family we've often needed to apologize to our kids, saying something like "It's important for me to guide and correct you, but how I just spoke to you was wrong. It came from anger and impatience. Will you forgive me?" When you apologize to your kids, you show real strength and create a space of healing and reconciliation that they can trust and emulate. Is there a time when your words or actions have wounded your child that you haven't yet acknowledged or asked forgiveness for? If so, take action. It's never too late to admit when you were wrong and make repairs.

As a parent, you will also want to come alongside your kids to help them learn to manage ruptures that occur with their siblings, friends or you. Sibling relationships contribute significantly to family culture. At their best, brothers and sisters provide support and encouragement to one another as lifelong allies. Still, conflicts between siblings are common and, when left unresolved, can threaten the health of their relationship and a family culture of love and respect. Teaching children to navigate conflict takes work. It may be tempting to silence the squabbling, judge the situation or prescribe a solution. But if you take the time to facilitate and teach conflict resolution skills, you'll be equipping them for a lifetime of peacemaking in all of their relationships.

When our kids were in grade school, we had lots of opportunities to help them practice making repairs. Noah and Isaiah shared a room. Being people with distinctly different personalities, this often led to conflict. One preferred quiet, and the other liked to play more boisterously. One was curious about his brother's belongings, and the other was private with his possessions. One would become annoyed, and the other would become hurt by the other's forceful assertion of boundaries. Some days the tension continued to build until it reached a pitch that included yelling, tears and physical exchanges—and we would need to step in.

One of us would call them together to (1) *stop and talk* then ask them to (2) *listen to each other* share their account of events. Since each person would get a chance to talk, we asked them not to interrupt one another. We might say, "Isaiah, tell me what happened. How did that make you feel?" When Isaiah was done talking, Noah would be asked the same questions. Sometimes they needed to go back and forth a couple of times to hear each other. And we asked questions to help them understand. "Can you see why your brother felt frustrated?" or "Is there another way you could have responded?"

Next we asked, "Are you ready to (3) *own your part* by admitting where you were wrong and asking for forgiveness?" Then we would ask them to (4) *give and receive forgiveness*. If they were hesitant to forgive, Lisa might say, "Look at each other right now. This is your brother, who you love. Your friends will come and go, and Papa and I will likely die before you do, but your brother will be your brother your whole life. What kind of relationship do you want to have with your brother when you're older? If you want to have a good relationship, you need to learn to love and respect each other now, work through this conflict and forgive each other."

Sometimes they were ready to forgive, but at other times they needed a little extra help breaking out of their funk. We'd have the kids sit on the couch with their hands on their knees and their noses touching. "Take as much time as you need, but I'd like you to sit here nose to nose until you're okay with each other. You can let me know when you're ready." It's hard to stay mad at someone when you're rubbing noses, and soon they'd wind up giggling and laughing.

When they were ready, we asked, "Are you right with each other? Are you ready to forgive and let go of the hurt?" If many injurious words were spoken, we would ask each of them to (5) *affirm love* by saying five things they appreciated about their sibling. Finally, we asked them to (6) *explore solutions*. Was something broken in the fight that could be repaired or replaced? What could they agree to that might prevent it from happening again in the future? A change may be needed, such as a new boundary being established: "Please don't wake me up before this time," or "I'll let you see my camera, but please ask me first." By modeling and teaching these six steps to making repairs, you can help your kids learn to be competent at navigating and resolving conflict on their own.

WELCOMING OTHERS

After we've hung the decorations on the Christmas tree, we find a seat, darken the room and plug in the tree lights. There's a hush as we admire our tree, hung with memories and warm with light on a dark winter night. We've invited the family who lives downstairs to join us as we sing carols by the tree. Their little guy is two and a half years old and loves to bang on the guitar and shake the tambourine. Watching him brings joy to all of us.

Over the years, many friends without family nearby have joined in our holiday celebrations. We were privileged to have Mark's aging grandfather stay with us one December. He loved telling stories, but after suffering many strokes, he had a hard time putting words together. So instead, we read stories he'd written down about his childhood aloud to the kids. "Grandpa Onas, did you really do that?" they'd ask, and he would nod and smile with a twinkle in his eye.

As you create a culture of belonging in your family, you can invite others into the welcome and warmth of your home. In fact, one sign of family health is when boundaries are permeable, when people can both enter and exit the family.

Welcoming others will likely look different at various stages in the life of your family. When our kids were small, we invited them to help us create a space of hospitality. We asked, "How can we make our guest feel welcome, comfortable and loved?" We would help them brainstorm questions to engage the visitor. Sometimes they created welcome signs or drawings. If the guest was staying overnight, we might ask one of the kids to give up their bedroom. We addressed any concerns our kids might have so they could be fully on board when the guest arrived.

Together we've welcomed young travelers on pilgrimage, older relatives and mentors, artists, activists and friends in need of extra care. Guests may stop in for a meal, sleep overnight or stay a week. One friend in need of a safe place to process her childhood trauma ended up staying a year.

When our kids were younger, it was very exciting for them to welcome guests, but as they reached adolescence, they needed more space and privacy, and we needed more processing time as a family. So we limited the frequency of dinner and overnight guests. Gradually our kids started taking the lead in hospitality, inviting their friends over for dinner, movie nights and parties. And we took on a more supportive role, cooking food and offering hugs and listening to a teenager who had a tough day.

Radical hospitality and care, especially toward those who suffer and struggle, is what made the early Jesus movement so revolutionary in the class-divided Roman Empire. As a family, you can strategize how to make radical welcome a reality. Who could you invite to join in the warmth of your family? Do you know anyone who's lonely or in need of extra care? Whenever you show hospitality, you extend the warmth of divine love to others. You communicate, "You matter. You are loved and you belong."

During the Christmas holiday, messages about "peace on earth" seem to be everywhere. But the twenty-four-hour news cycle, with its reports of ongoing violence, division and warfare, suggests that global peace is more a dream than a reality. We live in the now and not yet of the eternal reign of God, and we dream of the day when peace reigns "on earth as in heaven."

Jesus said, "Blessed are the peacemakers." Seeking harmony and making repairs in our families prepares us to become peacemakers in all our relationships. Peace on earth begins at home, and we wage peace by creating a family culture of love and respect, through a source of love that's greater than our own. Together we can create circles of safety, trust, belonging and peace that will one day rule the world.

A CULTURE OF LOVE AND RESPECT, BY HAILEY JOY SCANDRETTE

At their best, the words *family* and *home* represent safety, love and acceptance. Growing up, I was fortunate to experience the reality of these words. There are obviously many factors that contributed to making our home a safe and loving environment, but I think one of the most important was the way we learned to connect and communicate with one another. For as long as I can remember, there have been practices, rules and rhythms in place that promote communication, conflict resolution and connection in our family. We were taught to use "I feel" statements when addressing issues. We had protocols for processing and resolving conflict. Respect was expected from everyone and went in all directions.

Many of my friends have never had their parents apologize to them for anything or admit that they were wrong. I believe the concern for some parents is that if you admit to your children that you made a mistake, they will lose respect for you. However, ever since I can remember, my parents have been able to admit their errors and apologize for them, and they've asked if we feel wronged by them. I can honestly say that I have a very high respect for my mom and dad because of this. Additionally, their ability to so openly model conflict resolution allowed my brothers and me to imitate it in our interactions with each other until it became second nature.

As with our conflict resolution process, household rules were consistently modeled and explained to us. No rules existed "because I said so." The time my parents took to explain the reasons behind rules made me feel respected as an intelligent human who could be trusted to understand the whys and hows and not just the becauses.

Our love and goodwill toward one another was furthered in practice by mutual respect, trust and the tools we were given to address conflict and assert our needs. Affection, however, isn't solidified through intentional communication alone. Our parents took time to have fun with us on a regular basis. After dinner we'd often play games or music, sing and dance together. Sometimes one of us would be called on to share something we'd created or discovered that was exciting to us. My brothers and I always got along extremely well. Maybe that's partly due to luck and complementary personalities, but I think it also had a lot to do with the fact that family fun easily translated into sibling camaraderie. Even now, I'll watch TV shows with my dad and brothers a couple nights a week, and my brothers and I seek each other out to joke around and talk on our study breaks.

Our family culture is often hard for me to describe to people who don't know us well, because it's this intense blend of openness, mutual respect and understanding, willingness to get into the messy side of being in relationships and an affectionate desire to spend time together.

CHAPTER TASK CHECKLIST

- Choose a whole family activity to try that fosters love and respect.
- Talk about your communication rules, and practice resolving conflict.
- Reflect on where you feel vulnerable and how you are triggered by conflict.

REVIEW OF KEY COMPETENCIES

Connected. A thriving family relates with love and respect and pursues healthy ways to connect, communicate and navigate conflicts and have fun.

- We spend time together doing activities we enjoy that help us feel connected.
- We celebrate one another, express appreciation and say "I love you," and family members feel seen, heard and cared for.
- We have shared rules of love and respect that govern how we treat one another.
- We have effective tools for navigating conflict, making repairs, offering forgiveness and negotiating boundaries.
- Our family can welcome and invite others into our lives, including relatives, friends and new family members.

6

A Thriving Family Nurtures Growth

WHEN OUR KIDS WERE IN grade school, it seemed like all we did on weekends was go to birthday parties—sometimes two or three in a single day! We aren't really complaining; most of the time there were fun activities for the kids and good food and conversations for parents.

Riding home from a party one Saturday night, Isaiah suddenly yelped, "I'm about to be sick!" We pulled the car over, and he proceeded to vomit into the gutter. When he got back in the car, he looked awful. Like any good parents, we wanted to figure out what was making him sick. Was he coming down with the flu, or was it something he ate?

"Isaiah, what did you eat at the party?" Lisa asked.

"I had a few pieces of lasagna."

"How many?"

"Four or five."

"That's a lot of lasagna for an eight-year-old!" she commented.

"I also had some garlic bread."

"How many pieces?"

"Six or seven—and some brownies."

"How many?"

"Eight or nine. And there was a big bowl of peanut M&Ms, so I ate a bunch of those—and five glasses of lemonade."

"Isaiah!" Mark exclaimed. "No wonder you feel sick. That's enough food for an entire family!"

Isaiah began to cry.

"Hey, Spanks," Mark said. "You aren't in trouble. Why are you crying?"

Clutching his stomach he said, "I have to throw up again."

When he got back in the car, he turned to Mark and said, "Dad, I think I need to do an experiment in truth."

"Experiment in truth" is a term we use in our family to describe the opportunity and choice to grow and change. Isaiah had heard us talk about our own experiments and new steps we were taking to address problems in our lives. "I think I have a problem with eating too much at parties," he said, still pale and sweaty from vomiting.

"All of us are being invited to grow and change," Mark said. "When you're feeling better, we can help you brainstorm some new steps to take."

Life brings each of us many opportunities to grow and change. In this chapter, we'll explore how your family can help each other be responsive to this invitation. *A thriving family embraces each person's belovedness, holds their brokenness and supports their growth.*

BELOVED AND BROKEN

Family life often reveals the true nature of our character, the ways we see and respond to the challenges and opportunities of our lives. Getting married or becoming a parent can bring us into a new awareness of our wounds and brokenness. In public we naturally try to present our best selves, but our families see us at our best and worst, when our guard is down, when we're tired, sick, struggling or stressed. They see where our growth is being sabotaged.

This may be why so many of us have complicated feelings about our families of origin. The people closest to us act as a mirror, showing us what we're really like on the inside—and we feel exposed. We fall short of the love we wish to give, and our flourishing is threatened by anxiety, worry, anger, insecurity, jealousy, pride or fears that reside deep within. Each of us has growth edges, patterns of thoughts and habits that are simply not working, and these cause inner turmoil and external conflict.

What we're experiencing is the reality and complexity of the human condition, which is known by many names, including sin, the false self and the shadow. When faced with the reality of the human condition, we can choose to deny it, define ourselves by it or embrace it as an invitation for growth. At their best, our families gently hold our brokenness, affirm our belovedness and support our becoming.

Holding the tension between belovedness and brokenness is a tricky task, like trying to hold a needle-covered prickly pear in your hand without getting stung. Many of us have been pricked and paralyzed by shame. Shame describes what we experience when we fail to live up to a standard of behavior. It becomes destructive when we allow it to define who we are. Shame itself is not the problem, and denying it is not the solution. (Only psychopaths and serial killers live completely free of shame.) We can learn to interpret our experience of shame as a signal that invites us into positive growth and change. We hardly need to be told that we're broken or sinful; we know this by experience. It takes more courage to trust that we're beloved.

The truest thing about you is not that you're broken. The truest thing about each of us is that we are amazing beings created in the divine image. Life is a process of learning how best to flourish as the beings we were created to be—to respond to God's invitation to move from the kingdom of darkness into the kingdom of light.

THE UNWELCOME VISITOR

One of our goals as a family is to celebrate our blessedness and be honest about our brokenness so we can effectively grow toward our best selves—in other words, becoming like Christ in our character and behavior. We believe it's important for us, as adult family members, to model authenticity and vulnerability. We all have gaps between how we want to live and how we actually live.

Character growth is a lifelong process, not a one-time event or something only children need. Modeling honesty and vulnerability shows our kids that we don't expect anything of them that we do not expect of ourselves. Mark likes to tell the story of a character growth edge he faced that played out in the life of our family.

Years ago a stranger would regularly walk into our house and suddenly begin ordering people around. He spoke in angry tones, picked at small details and made harsh demands without listening. This stranger made life miserable for all of us, and we wondered, *Who is this guy, and why does he think he can walk into our house and treat us all this way?*

Eventually we began to refer to this unwelcome visitor as "Crabby Dad." You guessed it; I (Mark) was Crabby Dad. I felt ashamed to be so angry, impatient and irritable. When Crabby Dad made an appearance, I would often pray for patience and a change of heart. *Serenity now!* Yet it seemed impossible to turn my thoughts and feelings around in the heat of the moment. Eventually I would calm down and apologize for the way I had spoken to Lisa and our kids, but the damage had already been done.

After so many visits from Crabby Dad, I realized that whatever I thought I was doing to address the problem wasn't working. I felt stuck but wanted to change—to be a more caring, patient and gentle husband and father. God's Spirit invites and empowers me to experience this reality, but I needed to respond. I thought of something St. Paul said: "Continue to work out your salvation with fear and trembling, for it is God who works in you to will and to act in order to fulfill [God's] good purpose." God was ready to work, but I would need to cooperate.

I decided to do an "experiment in truth" regarding Crabby Dad—an intentional process of applying spiritual formation principles to my current struggle. I worked through the following steps.

1. What's not working? Where do I feel stuck? How do I want to change? I'm often crabby, irritable, impatient and angry with the people I care about most.

2. What are the patterns of choices that support the current behavior? At first Crabby Dad seemed to appear out of nowhere, but as I thought more about it, Crabby Dad was actually a result of a long series of decisions I'd made related to my thought patterns and bodily habits. Crabby Dad would show up when I was stressed out and overtired. Why was I so tired? I drank too many cups of coffee and ate too many sugary snacks, worked too many hours, neglected exercise, refused to take days off from work and stayed up too late watching movies, trying to relax.

3. What are the underlying scripts or thought patterns that support the current pattern of behavior? I had to consider the beliefs and thinking that drove my overwork and lack of self-care. Crabby Dad shows up because Mark Scandrette tends to act from the belief that his significance comes from what he achieves and how he distinguishes himself from others—from insecurities and false scripts about identity.

4. What is reality? What is the good vision of life God makes possible? My identity doesn't need to be contingent on achievement and comparisons. I can learn to affirm and develop a true sense of identity based on who I am as a beloved child of God. I can learn to be a loving and patient husband and father through a source of love that is greater than my own.

5. How do I want to respond? What mind, body and relational practices could help me cooperate with the Spirit's work in my life? I realized that if I didn't want Crabby Dad to show up anymore, I'd need to change my patterns of thinking and doing. Crabby Dad was no accident. I had literally trained myself to be Crabby Dad. My lifestyle choices were perfectly designed to make him show up. Even if it was virtually impossible to control Crabby Dad once he showed up, I did have control over factors that determined whether he would show up in the first place. I could apply principles of spiritual formation to my problem.

A spiritual discipline is something you can do that helps you do what you cannot by sheer effort or willpower. In the words of St. Paul, "I urge . . . in view of God's mercy, to offer your bodies as a living sacrifice, holy and pleasing to God—this is your true and proper worship. Do not conform to the pattern of this world, but be transformed by the renewing of your mind. Then you will be able to test and approve what God's will is—[God's] good, pleasing and perfect will."

6. What could I do differently in my mind and body to cooperate with God's good will for me? I made a list of limits and new actions I could take to say yes to being a more loving and patient husband and father:

- Limit my caffeine and sugar intake.

- Limit the number of hours I work and take at least one day off each week.

- Exercise four to five times a week.

- Have a regular bedtime and get eight hours of sleep each night.

- Develop a more secure sense of self based on being a beloved child of God by memorizing and meditating daily on Psalm 139.

I made a commitment to these changes in my work habits, diet, sleep and activity patterns and tried to adopt new ways of seeing and thinking about my identity. I'm happy to say that Crabby Dad hardly ever makes an appearance at our house anymore, which makes us all very glad.

Mark would be the first to tell you that his transformation was gradual, but it was dramatic enough that our kids noticed the difference, and it left a lasting impression: Dad is still growing and changing, and that means I can too. Hence Isaiah's comment in this chapter's opening story: "I think I need an experiment in truth."

When we enlist the support of our family to grow, they become our biggest cheerleaders and allies. Mark's story also illustrates an enduring principle about how change happens. We can train ourselves to think and act in new ways that are more accurate to the reality of how life works. This is why St. Paul once told his apprentice Timothy, "Train yourself to be godly."

Change involves recognizing the false narratives that drive destructive behaviors and trusting the authentic inner voice of reality that calls us beloved. Change also requires trying on new thinking, actions and bodily habits. Like a plant needs water to grow, healthy life practices help us tap into the source of life that allows us to thrive. This isn't merely self-help or a self-improvement project; it's an opportunity to respond to the vision of a life that's possible because of God's presence and the work of Christ, what Jesus described as the availability of the kingdom of God.

What we call an experiment in truth is actually an act of practical obedience, steps you are ready to take to surrender your will to the benevolent will of the Creator. Here's one way we tried to explain this to our kids:

> God reigns over all of creation and has good dreams for our lives. Each of us has been given a little bit of that kingdom to manage—your personal kingdom. Your mind is part of your personal kingdom. You get to decide what you'll think about and how you'll manage your feelings. Your body is part of your personal kingdom. You get to decide how you will move your body, what you will do with your arms and legs, what you will look at and how you will speak. Even your bedroom and toys are part of your personal kingdom. In that space you get to make most of the decisions about how your room is arranged and how neat or messy it's kept. It's a reflection of your power to rule and decide.

You can use your power to hurt or help, to heal or destroy—it's your choice. What's best for us is to learn to use the parts of ourselves to help and not hurt. St. Paul wrote to a group of people in Rome, saying, "Do not let sin reign in your mortal body so that you obey its evil desires. Do not offer any part of yourself to sin as an instrument of wickedness, but rather offer yourselves to God as those who have been brought from death to life; and offer every part of yourself to [God] as an instrument of righteousness." Growing up is about learning to use your power to say yes to what is good.

In our family, we're committed to helping each other grow and use our power to say yes to God's good desires for our lives. One way we do this as parents is by sharing our growth goals and progress during our weekly family meetings. This gives us a regular venue to talk about our challenges in a compassionate and constructive way. When we can be honest and open with each other about our struggles, we're less likely to try to fix the other person or be their conscience—because we know that we're both committed to taking our next steps of growth.

When appropriate, we also share our growth goals and progress with our kids, model the process and help them know that we're working on habits and behaviors that often impact them. ("I'm taking steps to be more trusting and less anxious." Or "I'm working to have a more healthy relationship with food.") The two of us also find it helpful to meet individually with a small group of friends we can check in with and, on occasion, to meet with a mentor, therapist or spiritual director to discuss particular places where we long for transformation.

 ## REFLECTION: EXPLORE PERSONAL GROWTH STEPS

One of the best things you can do for your family is to pursue growth and healing. Practicing steps of obedience, self-awareness and self-care can help you become a more present, caring and effective parent and spouse. Take some time to develop your own "experiment in truth" by identifying one area where you want to respond to the invitation to grow and change. Work through the steps below to develop a plan you are ready to commit to. Record this process in your notebook.

- What's not working? Where do you feel stuck? How would you like to experience growth and change in your life (such as finding better ways to manage stress, or navigating life without worry and fear)?

- What are the patterns of choices that support your current behavior?

- What are the underlying scripts or thought patterns that drive your current behavior patterns (such as jealousy, resentment, insecurity, fear, anger)?

- Imagine the life that is possible. What is reality? What is the good vision of life God makes possible that you are being invited into? (For example, I am God's beloved child. I have everything I need to thrive in this moment. Perfect love casts away all fear.)

- How do you want to respond? What mind, body and relational limits and practices can help you cooperate with the Spirit's work in you?

To experience growth and change, it helps to have the support of the people closest to us. Share your experiment in truth with your spouse or a trusted friend. Ask how you can support each other's next steps.

TENDING THE GARDEN OF YOUR FAMILY

Lisa is proud of her heritage as a farm girl and the fact that she hardly ate a store-bought vegetable until she left home at age twenty. She helped her mom weed and tend a garden—but not just any garden. It was a full acre of peas, carrots and potatoes that sustained their family through winter.

As we've raised our kids in the concrete jungle of the city, they've had a different relationship with growing things. Our small backyard is mostly covered in cement and shadowed by surrounding buildings. We tried to learn about growing things with a single seed planted in a paper cup and an herb garden on the windowsill. With the lack of nearby garden space, we improvised with regular trips to the farmers' market, noticing the seasonal changes in fruits and vegetables coming from the nearby fields.

When the kids were small, we joined a CSA (a community supported agriculture cooperative) that delivered a weekly box of fruits and vegetables to our house. Once we were even able to spend a night camping on the farm where the vegetables we ate were grown. The farmer took us through fields of heirloom tomatoes, Swiss chard and fragrant lavender, explaining how each crop is nurtured, cared for and protected from pests so it can provide tasty and delicious things to eat. Like plants in a garden, we are made to flourish, growing up into all that we are made to be and bearing fruit.

STAGES AND GROWTH

It takes an apple tree three or four years to produce fruit. And growth comes in fits and starts. Sometimes we expect fruit in each other's lives before it's the right time. When Julia noticed that her four-year-old son wasn't willing to share his toys, she was concerned that something might be wrong with his character. "I mean, he actually screamed when I asked him to share!" But after talking to a few other parents, she realized that sharing is an acquired developmental skill. She thought about what her son might realistically be expected to do right now. Then she came up with a plan. "I asked him which toys he was ready to share, and we put away the rest before his friend came over. No more tantrums. Yay!"

Every stage of life invites us to grow and change. You see this especially in the early years when a child learns to crawl and then to walk and talk. It's a big deal to go from diapers to big-girl pants or from sleeping in a crib to a big-boy bed. Motor skills and physical growth are obvious, but just as important are the changes we go through in our brains. Contemporary research suggests that our brains aren't fully developed until age twenty-five.

Psychologist Jean Piaget was the first to document the predictable stages of cognitive and moral development a human being goes through on the way to maturity. It's helpful to have a basic understanding of these stages to appreciate the growth challenges we face along the way. From birth to two years old, we're working on sensorimotor skills, and there isn't a lot of conscious thought or memory. Around age two, we discover that we're distinct from our parents, with our own will, and we learn to say no—sometimes very loudly. Soon after this, we start trying to piece together how the world works by asking, "Why?"

A teenager may go through a period of moodiness and withdrawal that's consistent with normal changes in hormones and emerging adult cognitive functioning. Even adults face somewhat predictable developmental challenges that may include a midlife reevaluation, menopause, an empty nest, reflections on their legacy and gradual acceptance of physical decline.

We can learn to appreciate and interact sensitively to the developmental challenges each family member is facing. What's appropriate at one stage may not be in another. A two-year-old screaming *no* is different than a seventeen-year-old doing so. A small child following the rules because he wants to be seen as a "good boy" is developmentally appropriate. But we would hope that an adult may choose to act from a more internalized sense of right and wrong as well as from a concern for the greater good.

Each stage of development has its own tasks and challenges. By being aware of what those are for all the members of your household, you can better support their growth and flourishing.

Personality is another factor that shapes the journey of growth. In our family, we've found it helpful to keep in mind that no two people are alike, recognizing that each personality has its gifts and growth edges. Tools like Myers-Briggs or the Enneagram can give you language to explore the uniqueness of each person.

In our family, three of us are extroverts, who get energy from being with people, and two of us are introverts, who get energy from being alone. This means we have different needs and expectations for social interaction.

You've probably noticed that people in your family are motivated by different things and challenged by distinct fears or insecurities. Maybe one person in your family struggles with anger and another with jealousy or perfectionism. The goal of exploring personality isn't to label, judge or diagnose but to better understand how to interact with and support one another. By being aware of distinctive traits, you can celebrate each person's uniqueness and more wisely invite and guide one another into growth. There's a path for each of us to become who we were made to be, reflecting the image of God and the character of Christ.

We were made to bear fruit, but not all fruit is alike. Just as it wouldn't be fair to compare pomegranates and tangerines, flourishing will look different for each person in your family. It's natural to have hopes for your child or spouse, imagining who they will become and what your life together may look like. But our ideas and expectations may not fit the reality of who they are.

Maybe you love competitive sports, but your child would rather spend time in the theater or art studio. Or you thrived academically, but your child struggles in school. It's important to keep our biases and desires in check when considering those closest to us—and this is especially true when a child has a developmental disability or a family member has mental or physical health challenges. If we expect fruit from people that they aren't capable of producing, we can wind up discouraging them. We can learn to imagine what flourishing means in light of who they actually are, rather than who we hoped they would be.

Though it's tempting to compare children with adults or to expect one person to be as mature or competent as another, we are each on our own timeline for growth. What's important is focusing on progress rather than specific outcomes. Instead of asking, "What do I want for my child or spouse?" it may be better to consider what fuller flourishing looks like for that person, given their gifts and limits. What new step are they ready to take right now?

ADDRESSING CHARACTER GROWTH WITH CHILDREN

"It's not fair! He always gets to do fun things, and I never do!" Isabelle exclaimed. She had just found out that her brother, Jack, had been invited to a movie by a friend. Seeing how upset his sister was, Jack tried to contain his excitement, but he couldn't help beaming.

"Stop smiling," Isabelle growled, "You're just doing that to annoy me! Mom! Tell Jack to quit smiling!"

It was time for a parent to step in to diffuse the situation. Was this an issue of cognitive development or an opportunity for character growth—or both? Isabelle often erupted with jealousy and anger when something good happened to her brother. She tended to make comparisons and had a difficult time valuing the good in her own life. She needed her mom's help and guidance to process her thoughts and feelings more constructively. "Isabelle, is it really true that you never get invited to do fun things? What about when Rebecca's family took you to see the *Lion King* musical last week? Good things come to you and your brother. You can choose to remember the good things in your life *and* celebrate your brother's good fortune."

It takes a long time to learn how to be a human being—to be fruitful and live well in the good lives we've been given. As adults we are still in the process of becoming, facing challenges and struggles as we learn to deal with the frustrations, disappointments and stresses of life. We're privileged to walk alongside our kids and coach them through this process, helping them identify growth edges. You can gently help your child see when they're acting from scripts that aren't true and behaviors that aren't working. You can help them cultivate tools for experiencing growth and transformation.

One child in our family struggled with being honest and truthful as a gradeschooler. Whenever this child lied, we would say, "Hey, you lied to me. This is something you don't want to keep doing, because it makes it hard for people to trust you." The message was that lying is a choice that doesn't work, not that the child was a liar. We took time to explore why this child felt the need to lie and what some alternative solutions might be. Gradually the child learned to make better choices, and now we have confidence that this person—now an adult—is trustworthy.

Sometimes we encounter each other's growth edges so regularly that we come to expect them, each of us playing particular family roles—the funny one, the one who's easily angered, the bossy one, the greedy one, the sneaky one. While these roles and reputations may develop out of true characteristics, it can be harmful when we define each other by them. We have the opportunity to think and talk about each other more flexibly, celebrating change and recognizing growth.

 ## WHOLE FAMILY ACTIVITY: CELEBRATE CHANGE AND RECOGNIZE GROWTH

As a family, have a conversation about growth and change. Parents, first tell stories about character growth challenges you've had and how you grew. Then invite each child to tell a similar story. Family members can also share or affirm growth they've witnessed in each other. Smaller children may simply share a new skill they've acquired: "I can tie my own shoes!" And you could add, "Yes, and I've also noticed that you were very kind to your friend yesterday when he was sad."

With older children or teens, you can take this a step further. Share about an area where you want to grow, and invite them to talk about where they struggle. Then guide them through the template for an experiment in truth—for example, "Let's brainstorm some steps you can take when sad thoughts overwhelm you." You can create a family culture where you're realistic and compassionate about struggles, and support each other to take new steps.

 ## FAMILY MEETING: TENDING THE GARDEN OF YOUR FAMILY

A wise gardener carefully observes each plant to address threats and provide care for each stage of growth. Each stage of human development has its own challenges. By being aware of what those are for your children, you can better support next steps in their development and character.

As we guide our children toward growth, the goal isn't just to address outward behavior, but to help them choose what is good and true from the deepest part of themselves. Take a few moments to identify a developmental task and a character growth edge for each of your children. Then consider what you can do to support their growth in those areas. We recommend making this a regular family meeting topic. Having this conversation together can help you get on the same page in your parenting strategy. Discuss the following questions:

- *Developmental tasks.* What do you notice about your child's current development? What challenges and opportunities are they encountering?

- *Personality and character growth edges.* How would you describe your child's personality? Are they an introvert or extrovert? What motivates and drives them to act? What gifts and challenges does their personality present?

- *Parenting strategy.* What are helpful ways you can engage and respond to support your child's next steps of growth?

PEOPLE WHO LIVE IN THE REAL WORLD

When we're in a wilderness area, we often remind each other to be on alert and keep watch for rattlesnakes, scorpions and black widow spiders. It's also a painful surprise to walk too close to a cholla cactus and its two-inch needles. We don't mention these dangers to scare anybody or because we're afraid; they are just facts that the members of our family need to be aware of to stay safe and alive.

This is true of life in general. Part of human development is learning to navigate the complexity of the world we live in, which mirrors the complexities within ourselves. Our planet is an amazing place of beauty and mystery, and as families we're privileged to marvel in and explore these wonders together. But we also live in a world of brokenness, pain and injustices that stem from the human condition and our collective actions.

Your family can learn to respond to the complexity of the world with critical awareness and compassion. As parents, it may be our instinct to shield our children for as long as possible from the harsher realities of life. But an awareness of complexity comes, and it's best for your child not to be surprised. By providing good information and being willing to engage topics, you can prepare your children to be wise as serpents and as innocent as doves—and you're far more qualified to guide them in this process than one of their peers on the playground.

Many parents wonder when it's time to "have the talk" about topics like sexuality, violence, race and death, and they wonder what the "right thing" to say is. It's probably best to think about these as ongoing conversations about life in the real world. Some topics come up because of what your child hears on the news, sees in a movie or encounters at school or in your neighborhood. Others come up because of an event that impacts them: "What happened to Grandma, and why is she lying so still in that box?" Or "Why is that man sleeping on the sidewalk instead of in his house?" There may also be important topics that your kids are unlikely to bring up.

We've tried to initiate table conversations about whatever our kids were becoming aware of or were soon to encounter. For instance, when they were near kindergarten age, we said, "So, you're probably going to hear people in your class saying words you don't hear us use in our house. Let me tell you what those words are, what they mean and why we use them sparingly." When they were in middle school, we started talking about drug and alcohol use. "Your brain is still growing, and alcohol is particularly harmful to people your age. If you choose to drink when you're older, here are some tips on how to do it responsibly." Or "Here are a few reasons why we recommend you don't use marijuana if someone offers it to you." In general, we've wanted our kids to know that Mom and Dad live in the real world, know what's going on and can be sage guides to living well amid the complexities of life.

We've tried to talk honestly and openly at their level of comprehension, not telling them what to think but teaching them how to think critically and compassionately. There are moral and ethical issues we do feel strongly about, and we haven't shied away from sharing those convictions with our kids. But we share the reasons why we hold those positions, and we try to represent the alternatives fairly, acknowledging that they'll need to make their own reasoned decisions. Here are some tips for having important real-world conversations:

- Decide what's important about the topic and what you hope they'll take away from your conversation.

- Consider how to discuss the topic in a way that is developmentally appropriate. You don't have to cover everything in one conversation or say more than your child can currently grasp. If it's important, you can bring it up again.

- Make it a conversation rather than a lecture. Ask questions and listen. Seek to understand why someone may think or act differently than you do, and don't assume that all family members see things the same way.

- Don't use language that stereotypes or labels particular kinds of people. Avoid straw-man arguments where you misrepresent and then refute a view that's different from your own. It's okay to express your opinion and views, but it's important to represent other perspectives fairly, giving the strengths and weaknesses of different positions.

Our kids weren't always excited to talk about certain topics—especially sex—but we would say, "This is too important not to talk about, so hang in there." If a topic came up that felt uncomfortable, to lighten the mood, one of the kids would say, "Awkward turtle," and gesture with their hands to show a turtle flipped over on its back and struggling to turn over and escape. Bursting into a smile, the other kids would repeat it. Then we'd keep talking.

We've noticed that many families have a difficult time talking about sexuality. Beginning when your kids are young, it's important to talk about safe boundaries around their bodies. A surprising number of children will be introduced to sexuality before they're ready and without their consent. We would like to think that this won't happen in our families, but it's more prevalent than one may think. It's estimated that one in three girls and one in five boys are sexually abused before the age of eighteen. Most of these instances occur with people the child already knows.

You can be proactive about training and protecting your child. In the unfortunate event that this does occur, having safety conversations ahead of time can provide your child with a healthy framework for processing the experience and seeking your help. Basic guidance about boundaries can be communicated even to very small children. Here are a few suggested talking points to include in your conversations:

- You are the boss of your body, and no one has the right to touch you in ways that you don't want to be touched.

- When an adult asks for a hug, you can choose to say hello or goodbye with words, a wave, a high five or a hug.

- If someone tries to touch your body in a way that you don't want, you can say, "Please stop." If they don't, leave and get help from an adult right away.

- Anyone who really cares about you will respect you wanting to keep your body to yourself.

- Certain parts of your body have special purposes. These parts, your penis or vagina, are used to make babies. They can also feel very good to be touched and were designed to share with a special person that you deeply love and trust when you are an adult.

- Sometimes an adult will want to touch a child's private parts or show their private parts to a child. This is wrong.

- I want you to tell me if anyone tries to touch your private parts so that I can protect you. If this happens, you won't be in trouble; I just want to make sure you're safe.

- Do you have any questions about what I've just talked about?

As they approach puberty, you want to make sure they have an adequate understanding of the changes that will happen in their body. During adolescence a person begins to decide how they will view and use their sexuality. Having regular and ongoing conversations about sexuality can help prepare your child to make wise and healthy choices. What do you want to teach your child to guide them in their decisions about how they navigate their sexuality? Here are some questions to consider about your own sexual journey and what you may want to convey to your child:

- *Sexuality is a sacred gift and a normal part of life.* What has been the gift of sexuality in your life? How do you want to communicate the positive potential of sexuality to your child? What do you want to teach your child about the physiology and mechanics of sexual expression?

- *Sexual expression has risks.* Where have you experienced or observed the negative potential of sexual expression? What are the risks and realities that you want your child to be prepared to navigate (such as unwanted pregnancy, sexually transmitted diseases, misuses of power, objectification and pornography, vulgar talk, emotional manipulation, sexting, harassment and unwanted sexual advances)?

- *Healthy sexual expression has boundaries.* How have you experienced sexual expression as a tool for enduring intimacy? What is the individual's responsibility in creating an environment for sexual expression that supports mutual respect, safety, deep love and trust? What kind of relationship do you think should exist between two people before they become sexually involved? What context makes it safe for a person to share the most intimate parts of their body with another person?

- *Developing a healthy sexual identity and expression is a process that takes time and intentionality to navigate.* What has your journey to developing a healthy sexuality been like? What have you learned that can help your child process missteps and potential feelings of repression, guilt or shame? How can you create a safe and loving space for your child to navigate their gender and sexual identity?

- *We can make better choices when we have a compelling picture of the best potential of sexual expression.* What do you picture as the very best expressions of human sexuality? What may a person need to say yes to and no to in order to pursue that vision?

Whether we're talking about sexuality or another difficult topic, the message we want our kids to hear and embrace is this: "Let's live in the real world together. We don't need to be afraid. Whatever is good, we'll celebrate and be grateful for. Whatever is harmful or hurtful, let's try to avoid. Wherever we see injustice and suffering, let's allow our hearts to be broken, pray for kingdom come and seek to be a healing presence."

RITES OF PASSAGE

On a cold and clear April evening, six men and three boys wandered into the woods to honor a rite of passage for our son Noah. Together they collected sticks, built a fire and roasted sausages. As the sun set and darkness fell over a eucalyptus grove, they gathered around the glow of a fire. "We are here tonight to observe the beginning of Noah's journey from boyhood to manhood," Mark announced.

One by one, the men began to speak—first Mark, then Noah's grandfather and then other men in Noah's life whom he felt known and loved by. Some told stories about the excitement and awkwardness of their adolescence. Each man shared affirmations, encouragement and wisdom about becoming a man.

- "Use your strength and talents to do good in the world."

- "Honor the person you may choose to marry."

- "Remember your Creator when you are young."

- "At thirteen, you're already so thoughtful, caring and wise. I am so proud of you!"

At the end of the evening, each person was invited to lay a hand on Noah's shoulder and speak a prayer or blessing over his life. Several of the men became emotional as they reflected on the beauty of the ceremony and the void of such a milestone marker and close relationships in their own lives.

When each of our kids reached the age of thirteen, we invited significant adults to help us mark the beginning of their journey to adulthood. Special foods were prepared, and each adult was asked to bring a symbolic gift or some words of wisdom to share. For her rite of passage, Hailey was given a tea party. Women who were invested in her life spoke affirmations and shared advice from their experiences. Afterward Hailey was presented with a book of their letters, which she treasured throughout her teen years.

Human societies have always found ways to honor the predictable stages in human development, marking significant milestones with a celebration or rite-of-passage ritual. Some rites of passage are rooted in a particular religious or cultural tradition, like baptism, first Communion, confirmation, quinceañera, bar and bat mitzvahs and wedding ceremonies. Others, like a driver's license, smoking and drinking ages, high school graduation and military registration are more civic and legal. And some passages are more personal, like parents deciding at what age their children can watch a certain movie, go to sleep-away camp, get their ears pierced or start dating.

In our modern and mobile society, which tends to be less rooted in long-term relationships, we've lost touch with initiation processes that have helped people journey toward adulthood for thousands of years. What are the small or large milestones you want to mark as a family? Are there particular traditions you'd like to create or celebrate?

GROWTH AS A LIFELONG PROCESS, BY HAILEY JOY SCANDRETTE

Growth is hard. As I've grown up, that has become abundantly clear to me. Being conscious of your personal development and striving to work toward becoming the best version of yourself is challenging and can be incredibly uncomfortable and scary. Despite growing up in a family where personal development was openly discussed and seen as a positive process, I still find myself fighting against the belief that the reason I need to grow is because I'm not good enough. I have to remind myself that this is a lie. Growth isn't important because we're flawed and unworthy; it's important because it's a part of life. Not only that, growth can be empowering, revitalizing and reenergizing.

Starting when my siblings and I were very young, our parents took a very intentional approach to how they discussed personal growth with us. They helped us to recognize the false beliefs that made us act out of jealousy, anger or fear, and they helped us to realign our behavior with the kind of person we wanted to be, as we were made in God's image. They supported our projects, interests and goals, which empowered us to see ourselves as capable of affecting positive change.

By providing us with strategies for personal development, emphasizing the importance of living with intention and creating a home environment where growth was encouraged and expected, our parents taught us that becoming your best self is a lifelong project. Now many of those tools and strategies are second nature to me. I have protocol in place that kicks in when I need to address conflict, calm myself down or make decisions, or when I find myself in new and challenging situations. I feel equipped with ways of thinking that allow me to make choices I will feel good about and to spot growth opportunities as they arise.

That's not to say that I do this perfectly. But it's helpful to feel like I'm not making it up as I go along. I have direction in my personal development, even when I'm in transitional life phases and feel surrounded by uncertainties. While it doesn't ensure that I always make good choices, the framework for growth that my parents gave me is incredibly valuable and grounding.

CHAPTER TASK CHECKLIST

- Reflect on steps you can take to address your personal growth edges.

- Have a family conversation about growth and change.

- Discuss your child's current developmental challenges and character growth edges, and brainstorm ways you can support their growth.

REVIEW OF KEY COMPETENCIES

Responsive. A thriving family embraces each other's belovedness, holds their brokenness and supports their growth.

- We're growing in awareness of our personal growth challenges, can share honestly with one another and support one another's steps of growth.

- We identify and celebrate the gift and limits of each family member's personality.

- We understand what may be age- and developmentally appropriate expectations for each member of our family.

- We focus more on internal character development than external behaviors or just following the rules.

- We're able to talk critically and compassionately about the aches and struggles of the human condition.

A Thriving Family Celebrates Abundance

WHEN OUR KIDS WERE SMALL, it was a constant challenge to keep them in the right-sized clothes, jackets and shoes. At times, they grew so fast they needed a whole new wardrobe every three to six months. While the children kept growing, we parents were working hard just to stay the same size or maybe even lose a few pounds. "What is the right size?" was a question we found ourselves frequently asking.

This game of finding the right size applied to all kinds of things, including beds, bicycles, ice skates, car seats and diapers. It wasn't just about sizes, but also kinds—the right kinds of books, toys and supplies for each child's interests and developmental needs. It was also about finding the right amount. When Hailey was born, she was given thirty-one fancy dresses at five different baby showers. How many frilly little dresses does a baby girl need? There were times when our kids had so many toys it was hard for them to decide what to play with. Once or twice a year, we went through each child's bedroom and de-cluttered to make space for what was now necessary and useful.

Life, in a sense, is a constant flow of choices about the amount, size and kinds of things that are needed. As parents, we have the day-to-day chore of deciding what's now too big or too small or too much.

But on a deeper level, we're challenged to consider this: *What is the right size and kind of life?* Another way of saying this is that we are in search of a life with the right proportions, the proper amount of time, money and stuff—not too much or too little, so everyone in our household can thrive.

We live in a society that, to a large degree, has lost its sense of proportion. The answer to "What's the right size and kind?" always seems to be more, bigger and better. The average size of a breakfast bagel and a new home have both doubled in the last fifty years. The results of this discontent are obvious and regularly reported in the media. The majority of us are in debt. Many of us are hurried, stressed or depressed. Most of us have drawers, closets or garages full of more stuff than we could possibly use.

We even carry our dissatisfaction in our bodies. Some of us can never be skinny enough, and more of us are overweight than ever before. Collectively, our outsized lives are making us sick, tired and desperate. It's curious that we continue on this outsized path, even though we know that this lifestyle is killing us and destroying our planet.

If we don't make intentional decisions about how we view and use our time and money, the forces of a materialistic and consumptive culture will make most of our decisions for us. Distorted beliefs about the right-sized life can keep us from the fruitful lives we were created for. In a rare instance when Jesus explained a story he'd told, he said, "The seed that fell among thorns stands for those who hear, but as they go on their way they are choked by life's worries, riches and pleasures, and they do not mature." The inordinate pursuit of safety and security, wealth and consumption can threaten family thriving.

To discover a right-sized life, we need to examine the beliefs and values that drive our sense of proportion and to adopt more life-giving and sustainable practices around time, money and stuff. *A thriving family lives abundantly, using resources wisely and practicing gratitude, trust, contentment and generosity.* In this chapter, we'll explore ways your family can thrive by discovering a right-sized life. Knowing that we live in a world of great inequity and ecological decline, we're also invited to ask, What is the right-sized life so that every family on the planet can thrive?

CULTIVATING A SENSE OF ABUNDANCE

When Hailey was five, she asked if a friend's family was poor. I (Lisa) was puzzled because, in fact, this family was very well off.

"Why are you wondering about this?" I asked.

Hailey explained, "Well, both of Zoe's parents work for money, and you get to stay home with us. So are we rich?"

Her question surprised me because at the time we had very little money, and I actually did work with the nonprofit we ran from our home. I realized that how I responded would shape Hailey's view of abundance. So I said, "We're well cared for and have everything we need. We have each other. We have good friends and relatives who love us. We have good food to eat. We have a good place to live in a city with lots of parks and museums and fun things to do and see—and we have good work to do. Yes, we're very rich." I went on to explain that her friend's parents were rich in many of the same ways that we were, but had simply made different choices.

That conversation prompted us to think more deeply about how we choose to see wealth and how we communicate that to our children. If we believe that we have enough and that we're abundantly cared for, our kids are likely to embrace this perspective as well. What if we choose to define wealth, not just in terms of bank accounts and material possessions, but also in measures of deep relationships, meaningful work and the simple pleasures of life? That's an understanding of wealth that can be shared by most people on the planet, rather than by just a few.

The teachings of Scripture offer a view of wealth and abundance radically different from many of the messages we receive from our culture. As Jesus once said, a person's "life does not consist in an abundance of possessions." Our lives are more than what we can own or consume. Many of us tend to wonder whether we will have enough; in response to this, Jesus famously said, "Do not worry, saying, 'What shall we eat?' or 'What shall we drink? . . . But seek first the kingdom . . . and all these things shall be added to you." It's tempting to put our confidence in what we can own and control, yet Jesus invited his followers to sell their possessions and give to the poor. What prompted him to make such revolutionary statements? What did he know about reality that we so often miss?

Do we live in a world of scarcity or of abundance? If we live in a world of scarcity, it would make sense for us to collect and keep as much as we can for ourselves, because we're in competition with one another. But if we live in a universe of abundance, where the Creator provides and the earth produces what's needed, it makes sense to give and receive with open, grateful hands—because we belong to one another. Nature and Scripture point to this reality. The earth brings forth food and everything else needed for human flourishing, and we're surrounded by beauty at every turn.

St. Paul's perspective on provision is also strikingly peculiar in our culture of more, bigger, better. He once told his young apprentice Timothy, "If we have food and clothing, we will be content with that." Elsewhere he said he had learned the secret of true satisfaction "whether well fed or hungry, whether living in plenty or in want."

Do you believe you have enough and that what you need will be provided? The ancient wisdom of Scripture dares us to believe that we have enough and that God's love provides all we need. Nothing can separate us from this love—not sickness or suffering or even death. Most essential to life is our connection with the living Creator, a more enduring reality than passing moments of deprivation.

Of course, these affirmations don't negate the fact that we live in a world where resources are hoarded and unevenly distributed. Because of this, not everyone has enough, and many live without adequate nutrition, clean water, good shelter, safety and access to medical care, education and jobs. In light of this, those of us with plenty are invited to share with those who presently don't have enough. We can choose to live generously from the abundance we've been given.

 ## WHOLE FAMILY ACTIVITY: PRACTICE GRATITUDE, TRUST, CONTENTMENT AND GENEROSITY

As a family, you can take steps to affirm abundance and embrace a right-sized life. Below are a few activities and practices that many families have found helpful. Pick one or two to try together.

Practice gratitude. Gratitude helps us reframe how we see our lives, inviting us to recognize and enjoy how we're provided for. With practice, your family can cultivate an attitude of thankfulness together.

- Instead of one person saying a blessing over a meal, go around the table and invite each person to share one thing they are grateful for from that day. Naturally you might include big items like family, health or a home, but also try to mention small things that bring you delight, like a favorite song, popcorn, your dog's playful companionship or the turning of fall leaves. Be as specific as you can. "I'm grateful for my family" has less punch than "I'm grateful that Isaiah made me laugh when I was feeling sad today."

- Keep a family gratitude log, a growing list of the things you're thankful for. Post it where you'll see it regularly to be reminded of the abundant ways you're cared for. Some families keep a seasonal gratitude box that they contribute to each week to open and read on Thanksgiving, or a chalkboard or table runner where family members are encouraged to write or draw what they're grateful for.

- Express gratitude for the part you play in each other's lives. "Thanks for being so helpful." "Thanks for making the great soup!" "I appreciate you washing my clothes." Try sharing statements of gratitude for each other at your next family meal.

Affirm trust. Even though there is much evidence that we're cared for, we still tend to worry. Some of us worry about safety and physical health, others about money and work, relationships or what the future may bring. We tend to worry about what we have little or no control over. Though it's a natural tendency, worrying accomplishes almost nothing. "Can any one of you by worrying add a single hour to your life?" We're reminded that the Creator clothes the flowers of the field and feeds the birds of the air—and that we're as valuable as they are. We can trust that our needs will be met, whether it's how we imagined or in some other way. When worries and anxieties surface in your family, here are some ways to affirm trust:

- Pray about circumstances that make you feel anxious, asking for what you need. Write down your concerns, and keep track of how those situations turn out.

- Remind each other of ways that you've been provided for through difficulties in the past.

- Ask for help from people around you, which may be especially hard for those of us who pride ourselves on self-reliance. Giving and receiving builds community.

In our family, when we've dared to "ask, seek and knock," we've often experienced unexpected provision for what was vitally needed: money for diapers, a vehicle for our ministry to kids and families, housing when we were once homeless. We have even encouraged our kids to ask about small things.

"Dad, I would *really love* to have a whole collection of Star Wars cards like Justin has," said Isaiah one day. He was often scheming about how to get things he desperately wanted.

Mark replied, "Isaiah, Justin's grandparents spent a lot of money to give him that collection—way more than you get for your allowance."

"I know, but I *really* want them."

"It almost sounds like you believe you can't be happy unless you get those cards. Is that true?"

"Probably not."

"I hope you can learn to be happy whether or not you get what you want. God gives us what we need and many other things we enjoy. What if you tell God you want those Star Wars cards, stop worrying about wanting them, and see what happens."

A few days later, it was Isaiah's birthday. During the party, as he walked toward the park with his friends, he found an entire box of Star Wars cards that someone had set out on the sidewalk for the taking. Now he had the whole collection he wanted *and* enough to share with his friends. This was a small concern, but the lesson learned was that when we have the courage to ask, seek and knock, holding the outcomes loosely, sometimes the results are surprising.

Express contentment. Being content is enjoying what you already have, deciding that it's enough and believing you have everything you need to be happy. In our outsized culture, we often convey dissatisfaction by accumulating possessions and compulsively spending or consuming. You can take steps as a family to express contentment by voluntarily limiting how much you accumulate and the amount you spend on discretionary purchases.

In a right-sized life, our possessions enhance our goals in some way; they have a practical purpose or bring beauty into our lives. When we have too many things, it can be hard to enjoy them all, and they take time and effort to maintain. Curating and editing your possessions can help you spend your time and energy on what matters most. Consider these questions to help you decide what a right-sized life may look like for your family:

- Are we enjoying what we already have?

- Do we feel overwhelmed by the number of things we have to organize and care for?

- Are there items in our home that we neither use nor enjoy?

- Does our space feel restful and welcoming?

- Does everything have a place?

- Does the number of things we have overwhelm us with options or provide us with just the right amount of choices?

- What do we need in this season of life?

Then pick an activity to try from this list:

Declutter. As a family, go through bedrooms and common living spaces one at a time, and eliminate anything you don't need, love or regularly use. Sort items into piles to put away, give away or recycle. This practice not only eliminates clutter, it can also help you examine why you acquire things in the first place and may prompt you to make different purchasing decisions. If a major declutter seems overwhelming, sort through or get rid of five to ten things a day until you have worked through your space, or choose a different room to work through each week. Focus first on your own possessions, rather than on those of your spouse or children. One parent has this advice: "I've found it easier to purge when I actually take the time to count how much of something I have. When I realized I had twenty-five dresses, I got rid of at least half."

Help your kids make decisions about their stuff. Krissy plays a game with her son called keep-or-give-away. "Everett finds it easier if we sort everything into two piles, rather than asking him to choose items to give away. We do this every few months, sometimes at his request—'Mama, keep or give away?' We're often surprised that he's willing to give away things that we would hesitate over, like a really cool fire truck."

Rotate toys. This can be especially helpful for younger children who find it easier to settle into activities when they have fewer options. Put away some toys and books, and swap them out periodically. It will feel like Christmas.

Limit the number of items in your space. Pack up some of your things for a while, and put them in a garage or attic. See how it feels to live without them. When the time you've chosen is over, talk about what you'd like to keep and what you didn't miss that you may be ready to part with.

Exchange. Adopt the policy that when something comes into your home, something goes out.

Be selective about gifts. If you want to reduce waste and save money, this is a great place to start. Some families limit gift giving to two or three thoughtfully chosen items, or they make homemade gifts for one another. What if a friend or relative wants to give your family more than you want or need? Try suggesting the gift of experiences or consumable hobby supplies. "You've been so generous in the past. You know what the kids may really like this year? How about a membership to the zoo? They just love going there, and I'm sure they'd love to go with you."

Wait before you buy. Purchases are often made on impulse. Have a practice of waiting a week before buying anything that isn't a necessity. When you're removed from the immediate opportunity to buy, you may find that you no longer want the item. To kick-start this practice, try fasting from discretionary spending for a week.

Pay cash and have your kids earn and save to pay for what they want. Give your kids the satisfaction of saving for the larger purchases they desire. They'll feel a sense of accomplishment and learn the value of work and saving.

Swap and share. Consider borrowing and lending with friends for things you each only need occasionally, such as power tools and camping equipment.

Live generously. Embracing a sense of abundance empowers us to use our money, time and talents to do good. We don't need to worry about running out of time, skills, possessions or money, because all we need will be provided at the right time. Therefore, we can give freely. Share what you have with others. Encourage your children to give a favorite game or toy to a sibling or friend who will enjoy it. Talk about how you want to give away a thoughtful amount of money. Involving the whole family in this decision can create excitement, as each family member envisions what could be done with those funds.

RIGHT-SIZED SPENDING

Like many couples, Laura and Jose have distinctly different approaches to money. Jose is a spender who enjoys daily treats and occasional splurges, and he loves to take the family out to dinner and sporting events. He is extravagant in his generosity and might spontaneously buy a vanload of groceries or a washing machine for a person in need. Laura, on the other hand, is a saver who carefully manages their family finances, stretching their dollars wherever possible to avoid going into debt.

For Laura and Jose, money is a topic that often brings up tension and conflict. The tension has only been magnified as their children have grown older. To meet increasing expenses, Jose and Laura take on occasional side jobs, but there always seems to be more things to spend money on: car repairs, sports uniforms, braces, an airplane ride to visit relatives. And now their preteen daughter is asking for a smartphone "because everyone else at school has one." Earning more hasn't magically solved their money problems.

Recently they realized that if they don't get on the same page about their finances, they won't be able to help their kids pay for college. They decided to sit down and develop an agreed-upon spending plan to help regulate their purchasing and achieve their financial goals. Jose gets a monthly "allowance" and has agreed to stay within certain spending limits. Laura feels more secure, because they are now saving for upcoming expenses. And since they have clear financial goals, it's easier to manage their kids' expectations and say yes or no to their spending requests.

A family, much like a business or a country, has an economy: the way resources flow in and out and a process by which decisions are made about how money is spent. A family economy works best when family members have a shared understanding of what resources are available and how those funds can be used to support their shared purpose. Learning to be conscious and intentional about our financial choices prepares us to handle the true riches of life in God's kingdom.

The people in your family probably have all kinds of ideas about how your money could be spent. But few, if any, of us have unlimited resources; so we have to decide what's most important. Clear financial goals and a realistic spending plan can help the members of your family get on the same page about how money is allocated.

A key to economic sustainability is learning to make work and financial decisions that are realistic to your current economic position. What gets us in trouble is surrendering to the pressure to spend to a level beyond our resources—in other words, when the spending decision isn't a right fit financially. For example, tuition, room and board at a private university may be a good choice if a family has the income and savings required. Making the same decision might be economically devastating for another family, if they have to take on significant debt. If your family doesn't have the income and savings to afford a private education, there are other good options, including scholarships, a nearby state university, community college or trade school. Some families can afford the grand vacation to Disney World or Paris, but you can also create lasting memories on a trip to a cabin or campsite at a state or national park. There's a good way to live at almost any income level.

FAMILY MEETING: CREATE OR REVISIT YOUR FINANCIAL GOALS AND SPENDING PLAN

Create goals. Family spending decisions are much easier to navigate when you have well-articulated financial goals. Ideally these goals directly support your shared family purpose. They may include things like reducing debt, buying a home, planning for college expenses or saving for a trip that will help you create lasting memories together. Financial goals that are in alignment with your family's shared purpose can help bring focus to your decisions about earning, spending, saving and investing.

Take a few moments to brainstorm and summarize your top three to five family financial goals. Discuss these goals, and write them in your notebook.

Review or create a family budget. Take some time during your next family meeting to look at your family finances. Are you on track with your yearly budget and financial goals? Are there any spending categories that need closer attention or new agreements about how money is allocated? A budget is simply a plan for how you want to use the money you have. The aim is to have a plan that accurately projects where you need to direct your resources to meet your financial goals. If you currently don't have a spending plan, use this time to begin the process.

If talking about money brings up intense feelings or conflict, take some time to explore why. You may be reacting to money messages you received in your family of origin. When Jessica was a child, her family lost their home, and her parents eventually divorced over financial struggles, which makes her very anxious about money. Daniel grew up in what he considered to be a poor family, so he strives to provide his kids with the possessions, experiences and status items he associates with the good life. Sometimes he overspends. He says this is because "growing up I got the idea that spending extravagantly on gifts, clothes and treats is how you show that you really love your kids and are a good parent." As you become more aware of what drives your view and use of money, you'll be empowered to make more conscious financial decisions.

TEACHING KIDS ABOUT RIGHT-SIZED SPENDING

You can invite your kids to appreciate, support and share in the economy of your household. Talk about work, earning and spending choices and the reasons you make particular decisions. We live in a time when basic knowledge and skills about spending, saving, investing and wise use of credit are scarce; many of us suffer because of this and struggle to recover. Increasing costs of healthcare, housing and education make it all the more important to know how to use resources wisely.

Financial competency is one of the best gifts you can give your kids to prepare them for life. Learning to manage resources well is a journey that takes time and attention, and your children will benefit from your discoveries and example. Don't beat yourself up about past decisions; just take your next hopeful step. There is a good path forward for you and your family.

Families have varying earning opportunities and make different choices about spending, so one challenge for families is how to navigate the comparisons. From an early age, kids often pick up on the differences: a friend has better clothes or a bigger house, or your family is able to afford gadgets or activities that their friends' families can't. When our kids have wondered why we make certain spending choices that may be different from other families, we've found it helpful to talk about tradeoffs. We spend less in certain areas because other priorities are more important to us. At times Lisa has found it helpful to say, "We could afford to go on ski trips like your friend's family if I got a full-time job or if your dad switched careers. But your dad and I decided that what matters more to us is doing work we love and having time to spend with you."

Kristine remembers an important lesson her parents taught: "When I was a teenager, I desperately wanted a forest-green Jeep Grand Cherokee, but instead drove our ten-year-old family station wagon. I brought it up often, until my dad told me, 'We could buy a Jeep every couple of years if we stopped giving money away.'" Suddenly the tradeoff was crystal clear.

Instead of saying, "We can't afford that," you could say, "That's not what we're choosing to spend our money on." This is a subtle but important shift from a message of scarcity to a message of priority; you are simply making a different choice so that you're able to spend your money on what you believe to be most important. "We choose not to go out to eat every week so we can afford a yearly family vacation."

We've found it helpful to involve our kids as much as possible in our family's finances, so that they can learn to make wise and realistic choices. We communicate our long- and short-term financial goals to our kids and share the amount of our yearly income, explaining how we use money to pay for things like the mortgage, food, taxes, utilities, dentistry, insurance, gifts, vacations and charitable giving. We think this has helped our kids develop realistic expectations about what we can spend. We may tell them, "We have seventy-five dollars to spend on your present. What would you like that's in that price range?" Or we may say, "We have a thousand dollars to spend this summer on vacation. What would you like to do?"

From the time they were in early grade school, we started giving our kids part of the family budget to manage themselves. This amount included a modest monthly allowance, their portion of the clothing budget, money we allocated for buying gifts for their friends' birthdays and part of our charitable giving. Each month we gave them this amount in cash or deposited it into a linked bank account. They were responsible for managing those four categories and, as they grew older, tracking their spending and bank statements with a ledger. If they wanted something that cost more than their allowance, we encouraged them to work and save for it.

You can start teaching your kids about right-sized financial decisions at any time. Sometimes the best place to begin is with the smaller and more tangible choices. Some years ago we went on vacation to see family in Coeur d'Alene, Idaho. At a waterfront hotel, we saw advertisements for a special ice cream sundae that was ten dollars. The kids wanted to try that sundae. We told them we had a certain amount of money to spend each day for fun and treats. Then we gave them a choice. "You can each have one of those sundaes, or we can pick up the ingredients at the store and make them tonight *and* use the money we save to go to the movies this afternoon. What do you want to do?" They chose the movie and homemade sundaes.

 REFLECTION

- What do you want to teach your kids about work and earning, spending, saving, giving and borrowing?

- What opportunities to handle money do you want to provide for your children? Will you give them an allowance or part of the family budget to manage? How do you want to involve them in your family's giving decisions? What do you provide, and what do they pay for themselves at this stage in life?

- What technique(s) do you want to use to help them learn basic budgeting and money-management competencies (such as jars for spending, saving and giving; a simple spreadsheet; a bank account, checkbook or debit card)?

After you've thought through these questions, have a dinnertime conversation where you share your thoughts on handling money, and introduce the strategy for learning you've chosen.

Educating your kids about the details of your finances can help them become aware of how much it costs to live and why you make certain choices about spending. Take some time regularly to have family conversations about your financial resources, priorities, values and goals. Communicate the details you're comfortable sharing with your kids. Here are some suggested talking points:

- Share your short- and long-term financial goals. Family members are more likely to be supportive of the considered choices you've made about time and money if they know what your life and financial goals are.

- Communicate some of the conscious tradeoffs you're making in regard to time, work, money and possessions.

- Share how much money your family earns and how much it costs your family to have food, healthcare, a place to live, utilities, clothes and so on. Pay particular attention to spending areas where family members participate or shape decisions. You may want to remind your kids that this is personal family information not to be shared with others.

- Talk about your family's commitment to being generous with time and money. What are the causes and concerns that your family is committed to support?

FAMILY THRIVING FOR ALL

Finding the right-sized life isn't just about personal financial sustainability. Consider making new choices about spending and consumption that are more in proportion with the limits of our world. Even if you can afford to remodel your kitchen or fly across the globe for vacation, it's worth considering what effect these choices have on our planet and future generations. We can easily picture the torn-out kitchen materials going into a landfill, where they'll sit for thousands of years. Or we can calculate the hundreds of gallons of fossil fuel burned and tons of carbon monoxide produced by the family plane ride to Hawaii.

What kind of precedent are we setting by the expectations we have regarding "the good life"? Do we believe that a person needs a certain level of luxury or comfort to be happy? Is this an option for most people on the planet?

We are challenged to find a more sustainable version of the good life that can be shared by most people on the planet, rather than by just a few. For those of us who long for things to be on earth as they are in heaven, sustainable living is one of the greatest invitations of our lifetime.

We live in a time when it's easier than ever to be aware of what life is like for people all over the world. Nearly three billion of us live on less than two dollars a day. And one billion of our brothers and sisters live on less than a dollar a day and can't satisfy their basic needs. Still, the top 20 percent of income earners account for 76 percent of all private consumption. The poorest 20 percent account for only 1.5 percent. If every person used resources like the average American, we would need an estimated five planets to sustain that level of consumption.

We're becoming increasingly aware of how all of our lives are interconnected and that our daily choices affect people across the world as well as future generations. We're invited to love our neighbor across the street and on the other side of the planet. As some of the wealthiest people in the world, we have the opportunity to make intentional changes.

What's the right-sized life so that all families on the planet and future generations can thrive? We can take steps toward living more equitably and sustainably by consuming less and redirecting our resources. Through intentional spending choices, we can help create demand for things that create better economies by purchasing products and services that rely on fair labor and good ecological practices. We can create less demand for cheap, disposable goods that wind up in our landfills.

This isn't a new way of life so much as it is an old one. Our great-grandparents likely lived far more sustainable lives. They bought sturdy items that lasted through the years, rather than replacing them for the thrill of the new. We can learn to value and preserve what's already made and make repairs when things break down. When something no longer fits, we can pass it on to others.

Previous generations also benefited from local economies. While we can't live exactly the same way, we can take steps to be more locally rooted. Perhaps you could drive less, putting some kind of boundary on the distance you normally travel for playdates and sports activities. See if you can get places you need to go by walking, biking or taking public transportation. Can you purchase some of your goods and services from local sources, like farmers' markets and locally owned businesses? Not only is this good for the planet, it also makes for deeper human connections and community.

Another practice that may be useful is limiting the amount of meat we eat. The average American consumes 195 pounds of meat each year, more than ever before. Close to half the grain grown and water used in the United States is for livestock production, which is estimated to produce 18 percent of human-generated greenhouse gases. By eating more plant-based foods, we can reduce the impact that meat production has on the environment. In addition, it can help us to right-size our own food consumption.

Finally, we can buy fair-trade and slave-free. Being willing to pay more for equitable goods will encourage companies to adopt ethical production practices that benefit workers. This has the potential to positively affect the quality of life for people struggling to sustain themselves. Fair-trade and organic products may cost more, but if you buy less overall, you can afford those higher prices.

For Kevin and Julie, moving toward a more sustainable lifestyle made sense but also seemed like an overwhelming task, given the demands of raising four kids. "Sorting garbage for recycling takes time," Kevin says. "And so does chopping vegetables for a meat-free meal," Julie added. But they decided to try one new sustainability practice every few months. It started with meat-free Mondays and learning to cook a few vegetarian meals the kids really liked. Then they started shopping once a week at the farmers' market. Gradually, they switched from drinking plastic-bottled water to filtered tap water. "Eventually we downsized to one car, a hybrid, and got solar panels installed on our roof," Kevin says with a laugh. "Over time I guess those small steps really added up."

Chances are your family has already begun grappling with issues of global equity and ecological sustainability. It can feel overwhelming to change long-standing lifestyle habits. But you can begin by taking small steps toward a right-sized life, so that your family, future generations and every family on earth can thrive.

LIVING ABUNDANTLY, BY HAILEY JOY SCANDRETTE

Abundance, generosity, frugality and resourcefulness—these words come to mind when I think about what my brothers and I were taught about money and stuff as we grew up. We were taught that our needs would be taken care of, that we should be generous with our time and possessions, that we should be wise and intentional about spending and that a little creativity goes a long ways in all these areas.

As kids we all had different tendencies in our relationship with money. I was always a saver. I love having money in the bank; I don't like to spend my last penny. This tendency was given structure as I learned to keep a simple budget at a young age. With my personality, it may have been easy to become miserly about my money, but instead the value placed on generosity in our family has cultivated my desire to share the abundance I've been given.

As an adult, it has been helpful to know how to budget my money and how to focus my spending in ways that reflect my values. It means I have money to buy gifts, to treat people to lunch, to give to organizations I believe in and to invest in meaningful experiences. While I may not have a lot of money, I'm able to budget and prioritize such that I'm not worried about going broke or being in debt. Careful spending and budgeting may not seem at first glance to be a spiritual practice, but it allows us the freedom to spend our time and resources on what matters, to pursue our passions and to allow God to guide our lives and purpose.

CHAPTER TASK CHECKLIST

- Do a whole family activity that helps you practice gratitude, affirm trust, express contentment and live generously.
- Reflect on what you want to teach your kids about handling money.
- Review or develop family financial goals and a spending plan, and start a conversation with your kids about money.

REVIEW OF KEY COMPETENCIES

Resourceful. A thriving family lives abundantly, using resources wisely and practicing gratitude, trust, contentment and generosity.

- We live with a sense of abundance, rather than worry or fear, and we trust that what we need will always be provided.
- We're grateful and content, we have just the right amount of possessions, and we are learning to distinguish between wants and needs.
- We have clear financial goals that reflect our values as well as a yearly budget to guide our spending choices.
- We actively teach younger family members how to handle money, and we model the wise use of financial resources.
- We're making conscious efforts to be ethical and sustainable in our consumption and generous with our resources.

8

A Thriving Family Supports Productivity

FOR YEARS OUR FAMILY LOOKED FORWARD to attending Maker Faire each spring, billed as "The Greatest Show (and Tell) on Earth— a festival of invention, creativity, resourcefulness, and a celebration of the Maker movement." Imagine an event that brings together robot builders, knitters and wool spinners, 3D printing inventors, steampunk musicians and food fermentors displaying sauerkraut and edible algae. The common denominator among these diverse participants is a commitment to discovery and to making things in a DIY (do-it-yourself) fashion.

At Maker Faire, there's something for everyone in our family to enjoy. Lisa spends time in the craft tent. Mark hangs out with the home coffee roasters. Hailey hunts for fashion treasures at the clothing Swap-O-Rama-Rama. Isaiah explores the digital music laboratory, and Noah investigates the Van De Graaff generator. At the end of the day, we come back together for the festival finale, when thousands of Mentos candies are dropped into two-liter soda bottles, spraying soda hundreds of feet in the air and onto the crowd.

Every time we participate in Maker Faire, we come away feeling inspired to do more for ourselves, to repurpose what we have or to make something new. We get a glimpse into the work that human beings are made to do: to tend and preserve, build and create and seek solutions to our greatest problems.

> "God created human beings;
>   [creating] them godlike,
>   Reflecting God's nature. . . .
>   God blessed them:
>   "Prosper! Reproduce! Fill Earth! Take charge!
>   Be responsible for fish in the sea and birds in the air,
>   for every living thing that moves on the face of Earth."

We human beings haven't always chosen to steward our creative powers responsibly. At times we use our power to dominate rather than caretake, acting less like makers and more like takers or destroyers. Nevertheless it's our nature and destiny to shape the world by our choices. We're learning to be good stewards of all that has been entrusted to us, using our power, imagination, work and creativity to heal and help—joining in the good work the Creator has prepared us to do. "To be of use in the world" is a phrase favored in our family to describe this invitation, and it's an invitation to all of us, both children and parents. *A thriving family celebrates each person's uniqueness and supports the development of skills and capacities to serve others and pursue the greater good.* In this chapter, we'll explore ways your family can productively participate in the work of the world.

OUR WORK IN THE WORLD

From an early age, we begin to look for ways to be a part of the work of the world. The two-year-old exclaims, "I want to do it myself!" We start in small ways, trying to button a shirt or pour our own bowl of cereal. We explore the work of the world through play, by pretending to be a doctor, teacher, firefighter, veterinarian, mommy, daddy or astronaut. Sometimes what we play or pretend becomes the real work we do as adults.

In childhood we begin to understand that we have the power to heal or destroy through the work of our hands. A little bird falls to the ground, and we want to protect it. A bowl breaks, and we want to fix it. These are early steps to discovering what is ours to tend, create, heal and protect.

We humans didn't create this world, but we have made something of it through our efforts. We build dwellings, roads and cities from the raw materials of wood, clay, stone and steel. We combine ingredients into a myriad of tasty food combinations. We sing songs, tell stories and make pictures. We clothe ourselves, not just for warmth but also for expression. We search for the best ways to manage our relationships and resources through law and governance. We create machines and make technical discoveries that have the potential to make our lives easier, better or more complicated. All this and more is the work of the world that we're invited to join.

We don't start our work in the world from nothing. Imagine how different our lives would be if every generation had to rediscover fire or electricity and which plants are poisonous or safe to eat. We've inherited a body of knowledge about how the world works and the systems and structures already in place. Part of the work of families is to pass on the collective wisdom, skills and knowledge of previous generations. And each generation has its own work to do—tending, creating, healing and protecting. Work allows us to live up to what we were created for: to exercise our capabilities as powerful and intelligent beings who care for and live in harmony with the rest of creation. We want purposeful things to do, and we want our time to matter. What is the important work this moment invites us into?

WORK AND COMING TO AGREEMENTS ABOUT TASKS

Work is essential to our survival and flourishing. In a family, a substantial number of tasks need to get done just to take care of the business of life: acquiring and preparing food, cleaning and maintaining a living space, managing household finances, scheduling doctor appointments, taking the dog to the vet—and the list goes on. Sometimes it can feel like these tasks get in the way of what's meaningful. Yet these details are integral and essential to our survival and flourishing, and they help us create a hospitable and nurturing environment for one another.

In our culture we have a tendency to see work and life as separate and to value paid and unpaid work differently. But common work can be a deeply meaningful way for families to connect and share life. One of Mark's fondest memories is of his whole family working together to clean up the debris from a roofing project. "For a grade-school kid, it was exciting to feel useful and part of something bigger—to work hard and then celebrate and relax together." Cooking, cleaning, shopping, chores, building or making repairs are great ways for parents and kids to spend time together doing real-world activities.

Work helps us develop self-confidence and builds capacity. When children do something for themselves or to serve others, their sense of accomplishment is almost palpable. Kids thrive on being challenged and are far more capable of learning and working than our culture often gives them credit for.

Building capacity is the process of transferring skills and knowledge from one person to another. You're probably familiar with the simple way this process works.

- You watch me work and listen to me explain how to do it.

- You work with me.

- I watch you work and provide coaching and feedback.

- You do the work independently.

Building capacity in your kids takes time and patience. It's not always efficient to have small people helping, and tasks take more time, but in the long run it's worth the effort. Sometimes as parents we may continue to do things for our children after they're able to do them independently—perhaps because helping makes us feel needed or connected or because we're scared to see them fail. But they need these opportunities to develop confidence and a greater sense of responsibility. Making them appropriately responsible for basic tasks is a tangible way of communicating "You can do it," and "I believe in you."

As our kids grew, we considered when they would be able to take on more responsibility. If we took the time to teach a task, they eventually built the capacity to do it for themselves. Contributing to the work of the family brought them pride and empowerment, and it prepared them to become self-sufficient and responsible adults. Beginning when they were quite young, they were able to help with picking up their toys, making their beds, setting and wiping off the table, emptying trashcans, cooking and running little errands to help a parent. As they grew, they learned to cook for themselves, wash their own dishes and clothes, clean the kitchen and bathroom, and pitch in with home repairs. Now they can paint a room, fix a toilet, build a wall and do tile work. Everyone can cook, and we love making meals together, especially homemade pizza. Lisa mixes the dough, Isaiah chops and browns the onions, Noah rolls out the crusts, and Mark and Hailey put the toppings on before they go into the oven.

In a family meeting that includes the kids, we look at the specific tasks that need to be done in our household and divide them between the five of us. Who has the time, interest and skills to do what needs to be done? Lisa manages our family healthcare, car and appliance repairs, tracks our spending, and shops for groceries. Mark cuts hair, does home repairs, prepares our taxes and directs the work of the organization that provides our income. All of us do some cooking, cleaning and yard work, and each of the kids has weekly chores.

FAMILY MEETING: COMING TO AGREEMENTS ABOUT HOUSEHOLD TASKS

You get to decide how you run your household. It doesn't have to look like your mother's kitchen or your father's car or your neighbor's yard. If everyone in your family is comfortable with a little mess, that's okay. If you like things neat and clean, great. But it's not likely that everyone in your family puts the same significance on each chore or has the same preferences for how your space is kept. That's why it's important to have open conversations about how work gets done, making sure tasks are distributed among family members.

You'll want to negotiate and come to conscious compromises where there are differences. Some families, for instance, make an agreement about how common areas are kept, but all family members get to decide how neat they keep their own bedroom or other private space. Or, even if it's not your preference, you may agree to make the bed because it would please your spouse.

Take some time to talk through your agreements about household chores, to discuss compromises and to explore ways you want to empower and build capacity in your kids. First, brainstorm a list of things that need to get done to maintain your household. Then work through the list and identify the person(s) in your family who will take responsibility for these jobs and when the job will be done. (Many families find it helpful to have certain slots of time during the week or month for these jobs.) Here's a list to get you started:

Job	Who?	When?
Cooking	_____	_____
Washing dishes	_____	_____
Washing clothes	_____	_____
Cleaning the bathroom	_____	_____
Cleaning the kitchen	_____	_____
Cleaning other common rooms	_____	_____

Job	Who?	When?
Cleaning bedrooms		
Taking out trash, recycling and compost		
Yard work		
Gardening		
Caring for pets		
Grocery shopping		
Home maintenance and repairs		
Vehicle maintenance and repairs		
Shopping for groceries		
Shopping for clothes		
Arranging haircuts and other errands		
Shopping for home furnishings and appliances		
Managing finances and paying bills		
Preparing taxes		
Managing healthcare (insurance, doctor visits)		
Coordinating kids' school and activities		
Transporting family members to activities		
Helping kids with school work		
Managing the family calendar		
Planning celebrations and shopping for gifts		
Planning vacations		
Generating income		
Other		
Other		
Other		
Other		
Other		

Discuss the following questions:

- Are we satisfied with how the work of our household is distributed between us? Are there any areas where it may be helpful to negotiate new roles or expectations?

- Where do we have differences about how our home is kept or what tasks are important to accomplish? What new agreements or compromises will help us live well together?

Consider how you want to empower your kids and build their capacity.

- What are your children able to do to care for themselves right now? Next steps may be things like self-calming, putting clothes on, getting breakfast, making the bed, bathing and brushing teeth or arranging their own transportation to activities.

- What skills is your child ready to learn, both to contribute to your household and to move toward self-sufficiency?

- What do you want your child to learn before they leave home (such as balancing a checkbook, shopping for groceries, using public transportation)? Make a list of desired competencies.

WORK AND VOCATION

There's basic work that we each have to do to care for ourselves and our loved ones, and then there is more specific work that we are called into by our individual passions and talents. Part of thriving as a person is the lifelong process of discerning how to bring your unique gifts to the world or how to discover your vocation. In a previous chapter, we explored how personality is a shaping factor in development and character growth. Here we suggest that paying attention to your children's personality can help you guide them toward the good work they were made to do.

You can become a student of your children, learning to affirm their gifts, encourage their passions and provide them with resources and opportunities that will help them discover how they were made to be of use in the world. Notice how they interact with others and whether they observe first or jump right in to new situations. Pay attention to what motivates them and when they seem most alive. Think about what interests them and what they're good at.

Over time, common threads may provide clues about the work they're uniquely suited to do. How can their natural abilities and cultivated talents bless others and bring good to the world? You can affirm the possibilities you see in each person.

- "You're concerned about including everyone—and this may make you a great leader."

- "You're so good at solving technical problems, maybe you'll use those skills someday to help solve one of the great challenges in our world—like developing better sources of renewable energy."

- "You care about fairness and justice. I wonder what you may do to bring more justice to our world."

- "You've always loved stories. I can imagine you writing your own stories or novels someday."

When most children begin talking, they start with words like *mama* or *dada*. Strangely, one of our son Noah's earliest words was *actually*, which tells you a lot about his personality. He has always been interested in understanding how things work and knowing how to do things properly—and he wants to tell you what and why. When he was three, while sitting in the kitchen in our 1890s Victorian, he looked at the ceiling and floor and matter-of-factly said, "Mama, our house is crooked." When he was four, he decided to teach himself to ride a bicycle. He peddled and crashed until he could, learning in one day without ever using training wheels. He was never very interested in toys. For his sixth birthday, he asked for woodworking tools and a toolbox so he could build himself a desk. His hobby in middle school was photographing birds, and he documented 150 species using a camera he worked and saved for himself.

Noah has been and continues to be an investigator, builder and tenacious problem solver. Throughout his life, we've looked for ways to affirm, resource and support his interests and passions. When he was fifteen, he had the opportunity to begin working as an explainer at the Exploratorium, one of the world's best hands-on science museums. For three years he spent time each week dissecting cow eyeballs and doing science demonstrations for museum visitors. This gave him the chance to interact regularly with scientists, and he was even asked to help develop a new museum exhibit. Through these experiences, he found out that he loves to discover the logic of the universe and share his discoveries with others. He now works as a physics and math tutor at the university he attends. As he pursues his physics degree, he's exploring where he may direct his research to help solve the critical problems facing our world today.

As you study and come to know your child, you can begin to provide resources to help them grow and develop. Actively involve yourself in their education, both in and out of the classroom. Think about how they learn, and support who they are. Offer further opportunities in their areas of strength and interest. Expose them to a broad variety of people. Introduce them to needs, and suggest ways to make a difference. Protect space in their schedule to pursue their own projects and interests.

You can use birthday and holiday gifts to support your child's passions. We knew Isaiah was internalizing our orientation to vocation when he told us, "I don't think I want any toys this year for Christmas. I need drawing pens and paper to help me discover how I am to be of use in the world—because I think I want to become a comic book artist."

A lot of families feel pressure to enroll their kids in as many activities as possible: sports, dance and music lessons, clubs and other commitments in addition to school. Many parents believe these experiences are necessary for their child to qualify for the right colleges. However, resourcing our kids isn't the same as overscheduling. One parent had this insight: "With four kids in our family, it doesn't take many interests for our budget and the calendar to explode. I'm starting to wonder if we have filled the schedule with activities but not with things that actually build into each child's unique interests and gifts." You can judiciously select extracurricular activities that fit specific interests and have clear benefits for your child.

We discover our work in the world through participation in real-life experiences. As a culture, we're just beginning to realize that our longstanding educational emphasis on standardized tests, rote memory and information is backfiring, because when not paired with life experiences, these methods don't prepare us for the real world. Only 50 percent of college students end up in the career they studied. That's an expensive way to figure out what you aren't interested in! One of the most effective means of discovering vocation is through real-life and work experiences, which can begin in middle school and high school through internships, mentorships, volunteer projects and paid employment. These experiences can either confirm interest or redirect. Isaiah thought he'd like to work with computers. During his junior year in high school, he had a chance to do a month-long mentorship at a local tech startup. Everyone at the company loved Isaiah, but through that experience he discovered that he's more oriented to people than machines.

Because paid work often takes a parent away from the family, many children grow up with only a vague sense of what their parents do. It's good for children to see their parents as competent, multidimensional and connected to the larger work of the world. Observing you at work can help them feel proud of what you do and to begin to imagine the work they may do someday. Are there opportunities for your kids to see you in your professional capacity?

We introduced our kids to the teams and people we work with and invited them to sit in on meetings and events. When possible, we took them along on work trips where they could see Mom and Dad in action. Our kids have had the opportunity to join us in what Hailey calls "the family business," helping host or set up for programs and even cofacilitating learning experiences. We also have a rental unit that everyone has helped repair and remodel.

SUPPORTING EACH OTHER'S PROJECTS

Helping family members use their gifts often requires the resources and support of the whole family. When Kate and Ryan decided that Kate should go back to school to get her degree in midwifery, they knew it would have an impact on everyone in the family. Ryan would have to take more responsibility for cooking and the care of their three children, and the kids would have to adjust to less time with Mom. Ryan says, "These three years haven't been easy, and we've all had to count the cost, but we try to keep in mind that this is something that Kate was made to do, and we want to support her in that."

When the resources and support of the whole family are critical to the success of individual projects, it can help to anticipate and talk about the costs ahead of time. In grade school, Hailey took acting lessons, loved performing and was invited to act in a movie that eventually screened at the Cannes International Film Festival. Her participation would require missed school and home chores, adjusted meal schedules, time transporting her to various locations and some late-night film shoots. Together we talked about these factors, and all got on board to help make her dream a reality.

We went through a similar process when Mark was invited to write his first book. The kids were aware that during the project there would be longer days for Dad, occasional writing retreats and less family time until the book was completed. During the process, Mark read portions of the chapters he was writing at the dinner table, and we celebrated lavishly together when it was eventually published. By involving the whole family in these projects, we were all invested in their success.

 REFLECTION: BEING A STUDENT OF YOUR CHILD AND SPOUSE

Think about the uniqueness of each person in your family, what their best contribution to the world might be and how you want to resource and support their emerging interests and passions. For each person in your family, write out responses to the following questions. If you are parenting with a partner, discuss your responses with one another.

- How would you describe their personality? What drives or motivates them? When do you see them really come alive?

- What are their talents, interests and curiosities? How have they changed over time? What seems to be the common thread as their interests have evolved?

- What kind of work can you imagine them doing? How might this kind of work contribute to the greater good?

- What tools and experiences can you provide to support their interests and passions?

- What education and career paths may be a good fit?

- Who can you introduce them to that could inspire them or be a good mentor or model (either in person or through media resources)?

THE WORLD'S GREATEST NEEDS

Frederick Buechner suggests that vocation is "the place where your deep gladness and the world's deep hunger meet." How can your energy, work and talents be leveraged to address the greatest needs and opportunities of our time? Families can help each other grow in awareness about the world's needs and support each other in engaging these needs with compassion. Here are some ways to cultivate awareness to engage the world's greatest needs.

Pay attention to struggles in your immediate surroundings. In the circle of your family, friends and neighbors, there are likely people who are fighting cancer, wrestling with addiction or mental health issues, or recovering from childhood trauma. It's likely that people near you are navigating the complexities of gender and sexual orientation or facing the challenges of being an undocumented immigrant.

Today there are few places you can go without encountering homelessness, violence and the divide of race and income inequality. Watch what your kids pick up on, engage their questions and affirm their concerns. When Isaiah was in preschool, he was particularly sensitive to the prevalence of garbage on the streets of our neighborhood. So Mark took him on walks around the block, greeting neighbors and picking up trash. What aches do you see in your extended families, in your close relationships or in your neighborhood and city?

Learn about global issues, needs and struggles. Daily news reports provide a lot for families to talk about and explore. And there may be historic, societal and global struggles you feel are important to investigate as a family, like global poverty, natural disasters, terrorism or modern slavery and other human rights violations. Books, movies and documentaries are a great way to deepen your understanding of these global concerns. You may want to say, as we often have, "We're watching this movie, not because it's going to be fun or entertaining, but because we think it's important to know about the reality of this situation. Afterward we'd like to discuss what we've watched." Follow-up discussions have helped our kids make connections between the struggle we've investigated and interests they have.

- "Maybe someday you'll work on a more efficient fuel cell to address climate change."

- "You could write a poem or a song that expresses how you feel about slavery."

- "I can imagine you using your people skills as a therapist or social worker to help survivors of genocide."

Seek places to engage. Look for ways to have firsthand experiences with the aches and struggles of our world. We tend to be around people most like ourselves, which can prevent us from being aware of the beauty and struggles in other communities. You can start by visiting a grocery store, restaurant or park in a neighborhood with a population that is less familiar to you. You may also look for places where your family can connect with a particular at-risk community, like a shelter or nursing home.

Some families can afford to travel internationally, but there are many opportunities to cross boundaries closer to home. Our friend Pam lives in London, and when she found out about efforts to resettle Syrian refugee families in their neighborhood, she invited her thirteen-year-old son, Jessie, to come along with her to the organizing meeting. It's most respectful to see these as opportunities to learn and join in rather than to fix.

Here are a few tips on ways to engage and serve as a family:

- *Explain what and why.* Before going into a new situation, take time to explain what your child can expect and why you're taking this new step.

- *Talk about safety and boundaries.* When our kids were small, we had a chance to connect on a regular basis with a group of neighbors living in tents under a nearby freeway overpass. On Sunday afternoons, we would bring games and instruments, food and a grill, to cook, eat and hang out with our neighbors. We knew that for the kids to have a positive experience they would need to feel safe. Before walking over to the location, we talked about safety and gave some pretty specific guidelines, like watch out for dirty needles and stay close to Mom or Dad at all times. Our neighbors always loved seeing our kids, and they often showered them with gifts from the street, which we let them keep if they could be washed.

- *Speak of people respectfully.* It's easy to want to put a label on someone who is different than we are. Mark unintentionally did this once, and Noah offered an alternative. "Dad, I don't think we should call our friends homeless. They have homes. Their homes are just tents on the sidewalk." It's important to avoid stigmatizing or labeling language. If you don't know what terms would be respectful, do some investigating or simply ask.

- *Reflect on your experiences.* After you've taken a new step to care or had a cross-cultural exchange, help your kids process the experience. How did that feel? What did you notice? What questions do you have?

Find creative ways to support and serve. Kelley, a parent to two grade-school children, explains their family's approach to this:

> We've tried to teach our kids that justice is about equity, about economic justice, about everyone having enough to live a viable life. We know kids in Burundi who don't have enough— not enough nutritious food, clean water, access to medicine or even school. Our family actually has more than enough, so our job is to share so that more people will also have enough, and we can all live viable lives. One day my second-grade son walked down the hall with an extra-bulky backpack. Upon investigation I learned it was stuffed with toys. "You can't take toys to school, son," I said. "But Mom, my friend doesn't have enough toys! I want to share my more-than-enough with him." Well, I could only bless him and his generous, justice-minded heart!

When kids find out about the struggles and challenges in our world, they naturally want to help. Here are a few simple ways to serve and support:

- Visit or bring a meal to someone who is sick or lonely.

- Invite someone who is alone or far from home to celebrate a holiday with you.

- Help at a local soup kitchen or shelter or with a park or beach cleanup project.

- Sponsor a child through an organization like Compassion International that does holistic child-focused development among the poorest and most at-risk populations of the world. Through correspondence, gifts and photos, your family can get to know someone in very different circumstances. Your kids can be involved in writing letters and contributing money that provides for nutrition, schooling, job training, spiritual guidance and medical care.

 ## WHOLE FAMILY ACTIVITY: NOTICE A NEED AND TAKE ACTION TOGETHER

- Brainstorm a list of needs in your local community (such as homelessness, loneliness among the elderly, someone you know with a prolonged illness, a community of people left out or isolated from opportunities and relationships).

- What are larger issues of concern in our world that you want to be more aware of and engaged with as a family?

- What is a next step your family can take to engage with this person or community? When and how will you do this?

RESPONDING TO THE INVITATION OF THE MOMENT

When our kids were younger, they often helped us welcome vulnerable friends into our home, joined us in serving at a local shelter and food pantry, and helped us put on awareness and fundraising events for concerns like human trafficking that we were passionate about. As they entered their teen years, we began to see the tables turn. Gradually they were leading out with contacts and ideas, and we took more of a supportive role, coaching them as they cared for friends in crisis or took up causes of their own.

After a devastating earthquake in Japan when Hailey was seventeen, she decided to organize a benefit event. She rented out a space, recruited people from her theater troupe to perform and planned a program and publicity. It was her event, but everyone in our family chipped in to set up the space. Lisa helped with food. Isaiah played his violin. Noah made cookies and set up the sound system. Mark performed a poem and took tickets at the door. As a result, Hailey raised a thousand dollars in aid.

Our kids are now guiding us into awareness and engagement. On the night the verdict in a nationally televised race-related police brutality case was announced, we were having dinner while news helicopters hovered over our neighborhood in anticipation of protests. Mark commented that all the posting about the verdict on social media seemed sort of patronizing—an example of "slacktivism." Hailey quickly challenged him, saying, "Yes, Papa, but aren't we called to be a voice for the voiceless, to defend the cause of the poor and needy? If we're silent, who will defend the cause of those who are being treated unjustly?"

Mark is usually the one making dinner speeches in our house, so Hailey's impassioned words got his attention. "Maybe you're right," he said. "So let's join the cries and prayers of our neighbors. If we leave now, we can make it to the rally."

We left our dishes on the table and walked out the door into the night. Marchers were just gathering at the Twenty-Fourth Street subway plaza, and we joined their call and response:

"Hands up!"

"Don't shoot!"

"What do we want?"

"Justice!"

"When do we want it?"

"Now!"

The hurt, anger and pain were palpable, visible in the hundreds of faces in the crowd. A young African American man made an impassioned speech, pleading for changes in a system that claims too many lives. He spoke with hope about a different and better future for us all. That night was the beginning of our family's involvement in vigils, rallies and petitions to end the race-related violence that persists in our neighborhood.

VOCATION, BY HAILEY JOY SCANDRETTE

I've always admired how my parents have been intentional and passionate about doing what they were made to do. As a child, I witnessed my parents doing their best to listen to what they were being called to do, and then doing it, taking risks and making commitments—like moving from Northern Minnesota to San Francisco before we'd found housing, starting a nonprofit, fundraising, living simply with three little kids to feed and making time to educate us at home.

My parents always talked to us about what they felt called to. My dad told stories about knowing, at age twelve or thirteen, that he was meant to be a leader and to help others live more fully into the reality of God's kingdom. My mom would assure us that making time to educate us reflected the passion she held for both education and family.

Mama and Papa also encouraged us to listen for our own callings. When they saw us drawn to something, they'd ask us about it, commenting that they could imagine us living out our purpose through that passion. This trained me to notice what made me feel most alive and in touch with God and the world around me.

I knew from a very early age that I wanted to work with people, helping, leading and healing. Sometimes I worried that my interest in theater or writing wasn't doing enough to help or heal, but my parents encouraged me that, in doing whatever I was created to do, I would find ways to bring love to people. Their encouragement was underlined by their actions, as I watched them using their gifts to serve.

Having this modeled for me from such a young age has been incredibly valuable. It empowered me to choose a college major I'm passionate about, rather than one that will be potentially lucrative, and I feel supported in that choice. I hear many of my peers say things like "I just want to work a job I like and to make enough money to live." But to me, following my vocational path is so much more than finding a job I like; it's answering the call to seek meaning and greater wholeness through the work I do, doing my part to bring the love and light of the Creator into the world.

CHAPTER TASK CHECKLIST

- Talk about the work that needs to get done in your family and how your children can learn and help.

- Reflect on the personality and passions of each person in your family and how you can support each other's development.

- Try an activity that helps your family compassionately engage the aches and opportunities of our world.

REVIEW OF KEY COMPETENCIES

Productive. A thriving family celebrates each person's uniqueness and supports the development of skills and capacities to serve others and pursue the greater good.

- We help identify, nurture and celebrate the gifts of each family member and help each other imagine how our gifts and skills can best serve others.

- We resource the development of skills and capacities to help family members make a meaningful contribution to society.

- We model and teach the dignity and value of work, diligence and a job well done.

- We're helping each other discover how to compassionately engage the great aches and opportunities in our world.

- We take steps to practice compassion and serve together as a family.

Conclusion

THROUGHOUT THIS BOOK, we've explored perspectives and practices that can help your family create a thriving family culture. We're grateful you made the investment and took the time to read these pages, and we trust you've been able to take new steps to reflect, connect and act as a family. Congratulations! Know that every step your family takes to live intentionally will be rewarded.

Writing this book has given us a wonderful opportunity to reflect on the best of what we've experienced and learned over the past twenty-five years of life together as a family. We trust we've written with enough honesty for you to know that, like you, we've had our share of hard days, personal challenges and regrets—as well as much to celebrate. If after reading this book you feel even slightly overwhelmed by the gap between the family you are and the family you want to be, remember that pursuing family belonging and becoming is a lifelong process. Small steps and sustained effort, over time, will make a big difference. Regularly practicing and maintaining the three core tools utilized in this book—reflection, family meetings and family activities—can help you keep momentum.

After using the tools and practices in this book, one couple commented, "This process helped us have many important conversations about the family we want to be. The tools have been helpful, and we're excited about the family purpose agreement we developed. But we're also a little afraid that we're going to forget everything and go back to our old patterns."

To keep momentum in your shared purpose, we encourage you to focus on a few concrete steps and priorities. Here's an approach we've found helpful. Once a year, as a couple we have a "state of the union" conversation about our family, usually around New Year's Day. We take a long walk along the Marina Green, a beautiful path that leads to the Golden Gate Bridge. As we walk, we reflect on the past year, first by asking, "What can we celebrate? How are we living into our shared family purpose?" Usually one of us takes notes, and we make a list. Here's our list from a few years ago:

- Noah graduated from high school and was accepted to college.
- Successful launch of our *Free* book project.
- Great time connecting as a family on our vacation to the Pacific Northwest.
- Important house repairs completed, including resurfacing hardwood floors.

Then we ask each other, "What's not working? What are the challenges and difficulties our family is facing right now?"

- Fatigue from frequent travel and an intense schedule.
- Worry and anxiety about our kids' transitions from high school to college.
- Increased conflict in our relationship.
- Adjusting to new schedules and dynamics with everyone entering new life stages.

Then we ask each other, "How would you like the next year to feel different?"

- Deeper care and connection in our marriage.
- Better work/life balance and more time in nature.

- Increased fitness, health and stamina.
- More peace about life transitions.

And finally, we set some priorities for the coming year by asking, "What are the five most important goals we could pursue in the next year to help us live into our shared purpose?"

1. Find new ways to partner on projects (such as the book you're reading) and travel together.

2. Take intentional steps to lower anxiety, affirm trust and navigate transitions.

3. Focus on daily practices that will help us have better fitness, health and stamina.

4. Complete home repairs, and make purchases to be more prepared to offer hospitality.

5. Make next-step financial decisions, and investigate solar power installation.

Then, as a whole family, we have a similar "state of the union" conversation. In our family meetings, we check in on the priorities we set for the year and make strategic plans for accomplishing those goals.

So, before you set this book down, we encourage you to have a "state of the union" conversation about your family and set concrete priorities for the next year.

- What can you celebrate? How are you living into your shared family purpose?
- What's not working? What are the challenges your family is facing right now?
- How would you like the next year to feel different?
- What five priorities will help you move forward in your family purpose over the next year?

AS STRONG AS A FOREST

The remaining redwood groves along the California coast hold a captivating allure, especially near sunset, when sunlight, filtered through fog, dances with lengthening shadows. Walking among these ancient trees, one is conscious of the sacredness of life and the mystery of time. The impact of this scene is not a single tree, but the beauty of the whole forest.

Similarly, our families, linked together, make up a flourishing landscape. We trust that your family will seek supportive companions for this journey. We need each other to grow strong and prosper from generation to generation. Together, may we be receptive to the Creator's energy, united by shared purpose, rooted in healthful rhythms, connected through love and respect, responsive to the invitation to grow, living abundantly and working together for the greater good, so that all families on earth can thrive.

Acknowledgments

MANY THANKS TO THE FOCUS GROUP participants and early readers who provided valuable feedback on the manuscript and who generously shared stories from their own family experiences: Tobi Rouse, Pete and Jackie Bulanow and Mike Stavlund (Common Table, Washington, DC), Meredith Miller (Willow Creek Community Church, South Barrington, Illinois), Charley Scandlyn (Menlo Church, Menlo Park, California), Dave and Krissy Kludt (Open Door Community, Walnut Creek, California), Jarrod and Taryn Shappell (San Francisco), Char and Keith Klassen (Sacramento), Denise Eide (Pedia Learning, Inc.), Alex and Amy Schweng (Missio Dei, Oakland, California), Missy Neumeyer (Duluth, Minnesota) and Kelley Johnson Nikondeha (Communities of Hope, Burundi, Africa).

Thanks also to the groups that provided forums for us to refine the content of this book through retreats, workshops and other teaching opportunities: Wild Goose Festival, Manhattan Beach Community Church (Manhattan Beach, California), The Neighborhood Church (Palos Verdes, California), The Orchard Community (Aurora, Illinois), GRX Church (Fremont, California), InnerChange (London) and The Faith Forward Conference for children and youth ministry leaders (Chicago).

We are grateful for the assistance of our literary agent, Greg Daniels, and our partnership with InterVarsity Press, especially our editor Cindy Bunch and the marketing team led by Andrew Bronson.

Thanks to Mark's parents, Rich and Barb Scandrette, who value the gift and importance of family, live with great intentionality and have modeled so many of the skills and competencies explored in this book. And thanks to Lisa's parents, Jim and Sue Sands, who provided an atmosphere of warmth and hospitality to so many, generously caring for family from one generation to the next.

Special thanks to Hailey Scandrette for her reflections on our family experience.

We appreciate the wonderful opportunity writing this book gave us to reflect on our family experience as our kids transitioned into early adulthood. We are thankful for one another's trust, patience and laughter during this process as well as the divine grace and guidance provided.

Group Learning Guide

Working through the steps in this book with a group of people can provide the solidarity and support needed for lasting change and can create a profound sense of community and trust among participants. Here are a few tips for initiating and leading a group to work through the tasks and exercises in *Belonging and Becoming*.

LEADERSHIP

Form a team of two to three people who will initiate the learning group and facilitate sessions. We can't stress enough how important it is to have collaborators in this process. When you collaborate, you have a greater pool of skills and wisdom to draw from and a wider network of potential participants to invite.

Decide together when and where you will meet, how you'll invite participants and the roles each person will play during your group sessions. People in your group will be only as invested and authentic as the facilitators are. The honesty, self-awareness and commitment to growth and change you model will set the tone for the entire group. Make sure your core team has the time and space necessary to facilitate this process.

INVITATION

As you invite people into the learning group, make the opportunity and expectations for participation clear. You're inviting participants into an intensive and practical process of cultivating skills for creating a thriving family culture. Participants will get the most out of this experience if you set the expectation that this is a high-commitment learning journey rather than a book study. If you're introducing this opportunity to an existing group that meets regularly for other purposes, emphasize the unique intensity and commitment to action this process will require.

Participants will get the most out of this experience by making a commitment to participate fully in the process by attending all sessions, reading the assigned chapter and completing tasks and exercises before the next session. To solidify this commitment, invite participants to sign the Shared Learning Contract at your first session. Here are a few things to keep in mind as you invite people to participate:

- The main purpose of this eight-session intensive is to develop skills for taking practical steps to create a thriving family culture.

- For momentum and group safety, it's important to attend every session and not to allow new people into the group after the first week.

- The time commitment required includes a one- to two-hour group meeting, and three hours to read the chapter and do chapter tasks before the next session.

- Don't be surprised if a few people decline your invitation or drop out partway through. It's common for 5 to 10 percent of a group to drop out within the first two weeks of a high-intensity process like this.

SESSION FACILITATION

Create a welcoming, conversational and supportive environment. Your willingness to risk honesty and transparency about your successes and failures will empower others to do the same. Try to include everyone in conversations. Invite less talkative people to respond to questions, and gently redirect over-talkers by saying something like "Okay, now let's hear from someone who hasn't had a chance to share yet." Be creative, and make your group experience fun, lively and unpredictable. Each session is designed to include the following elements:

- a welcome and opening prayer
- discussion of some aspect of the assigned chapter
- a check-in on the exercises, tasks and experiments of the assigned chapter (done in smaller huddle groups of three to four people)
- a suggested Scripture to engage with as a group
- a group exercise that explores a theme from the chapter
- a review of chapter tasks to complete before the next session
- a closing meditation or prayer

Plan activities for the session ahead of time. The Group Learning Guide includes ninety minutes of activities. Estimated times for specific session activities are provided but flexible; expect them to take slightly more or less time, depending on the dynamics of your group.

If possible, allow two hours to meet, including fifteen minutes of socializing before and after session activities. You can shorten your session to an hour by eliminating some of the suggested activities, but most groups who've gone through this process say they could always use more time to process the steps they're taking.

As you look at the guide for each session, decide what activities are most relevant to your group. There may be more suggested activities than you have time for.

Enter each session assuming participants have done the chapter tasks. Always include check-in, and review what to do before the next session. These are important elements of the learning process, providing accountability and support for new steps of action. If there are more than five people in your group, we recommend dividing up into "huddles" of three to four people to check in on homework tasks. Designate a facilitator for each huddle. To ensure that each person in the huddle has the opportunity to share, try using a timer. Give each person in the huddle group a certain amount of time to check in on homework tasks.

Many of the topics brought up in this process lead to emotional sharing. Be prepared to care for and walk alongside people as they face regrets, new realizations and invitations to greater freedom and healing. Some people in your group may need more space to process outside of group sessions or assistance in completing tasks and exercises.

Think about who is in the room. Consider their ages, life stages and circumstances. Choose activities and discussion topics that are relevant to the people in your circle.

Not everyone has the same strengths or growth edges when it comes to this process. You may need to speak up for an underrepresented perspective occasionally so that each participant's life experience is acknowledged.

Regularly remind your group of the vision and goals of the group process. Some people will be taking courageous and challenging new steps in their lives. With the effort required, sometimes it's easy to forget the "why" for specific tasks or activities. The tasks and exercises for each session are designed to help participants take their next step toward family thriving.

Follow up your weekly session with an email to participants. After each session, send a note that summarizes the discussion, offers encouragement and reminds participants of the tasks to complete before the next session.

Near the end of your process, invite the group to consider what's next. Walking through the steps in this book together can lead to a strong sense of community and trust. The group may want to consider ways to stay connected on a monthly or quarterly basis to keep on track with their commitments and steps to growth.

SESSION 1: A THRIVING FAMILY
LIVES FROM A VISION

Before this session: Read chapter 1, and complete the Family Thriving Self-Assessment.

Session goals

- Help each other feel welcome and connected, and take steps to build trust.
- Reflect on the invitation into a flourishing life of belonging and becoming.
- Value family strengths and help each other identify growth areas.
- Review and sign the Shared Learning Contract.

Welcome (10 minutes)

- Invite each person to introduce themselves, and briefly answer the following questions:
  - What do you like about the family you're part of?
  - What do you hope to gain from this group learning experience?

Prayer (2 minutes)

Read the "Group Prayer for Family Thriving" together.

Chapter discussion (15 minutes)

- What resonated with you from chapter 1?
- What questions do you have about the process of creating a thriving family culture?
- Do you have any triggers or baggage around this topic? How can this group help you stay open to the process?

Scripture (10 minutes)

Read the following words of Jesus three times aloud, pausing after each reading to invite group members to offer a one-word response to the questions below.

> *"Come to me, all you who are weary and burdened, and I will give you rest. Take my yoke upon you and learn from me, for I am gentle and humble in heart, and you will find rest for your souls. For my yoke is easy and my burden is light."*

- Family life can be tiring and difficult at times. What is one word you would use to describe an aspect of family life that makes you feel weary or burdened?

- The Creator invites us into the potential of true rest. What is a word that describes the thriving you desire for your family?

- Jesus invites us to learn from him. What do you want the master to teach you that will help you and your family flourish? Respond by completing this sentence: "I want to learn to . . ."

Chapter task check-in (30 minutes)

Invite each person to take seven to ten minutes to complete the Family Thriving Self-Assessment (p. 27-31) and then reflect together on the results. If your group is larger than five people, divide into groups of three or four to do this activity. Take turns responding to the following questions, allowing each person five minutes to share. You may find it useful to use a timer to keep your group on track.

- What did you identify as your family's greatest areas of strength? Why?

- Which of these did you identify as your greatest area for growth? Explain.

- Prior to this session, did you get a chance to engage your spouse and other family members in an activity to explore what you like about your family? How was that interaction?

Shared Learning Contract (5 minutes)

- Read, briefly discuss and then sign the Shared Learning Contract (p. 228-228).

- Make sure you have contact information for each participant so you can be in communication between sessions.

Announce and explain homework tasks (5 minutes)

- Read chapter 2.
- Reflect on your family-of-origin experience and scripts.
- Develop a family purpose agreement.
- Do an activity that invites your children to engage with your family purpose agreement.

Closing prayer (2 minutes)

Read the "Group Prayer for Family Thriving" once more together.

SESSION 2: A THRIVING FAMILY CARRIES OUT ITS PURPOSE

Session goals

- Reflect on family-of-origin experiences.
- Explore the gifts and shadows of the scripts that shape how you approach family life.
- Affirm one another's family purpose agreements.

Welcome and prayer (5 minutes)

Gather as a group, and invite each other into two minutes of silence before reading the "Group Prayer for Family Thriving."

Chapter discussion (10 minutes)

- What stood out to you as you read this chapter on family purpose?
- Has this process brought up any interesting conversations in your family?

Scripture (10 minutes)

Read the following passages from Psalms responsively. Invite one person to read each section, and then have the whole group respond with the italicized refrain. (This is also a great way to invite kids to engage with psalms.)

> Lord, you have been our dwelling place
> throughout all generations.
> Before the mountains were born
> or you brought forth the whole world,
> from everlasting to everlasting you are God.
> *Lord, you have been our dwelling place throughout all generations.*
> You turn people back to dust,
> saying, "Return to dust, you mortals."
> A thousand years in your sight
> are like a day that has just gone by,
> or like a watch in the night.
> *Lord, you have been our dwelling place throughout all generations.*
> Yet you sweep people away in the sleep of death—
> they are like the new grass of the morning:
> In the morning it springs up new,
> but by evening it's dry and withered. . . .
> *Lord, you have been our dwelling place throughout all generations.*
> Teach us to number our days,
> that we may gain a heart of wisdom.
> Relent, LORD! How long will it be?
> Have compassion on your servants.
> *Lord, you have been our dwelling place throughout all generations.*
> Satisfy us in the morning with your unfailing love,
> that we may sing for joy and be glad all our days.
> Make us glad for as many days as you have afflicted us,
> for as many years as we have seen trouble.
> *Lord, you have been our dwelling place throughout all generations.*
> May your deeds be shown to your servants,
> your splendor to their children.
> May the favor of the Lord our God rest on us;

establish the work of our hands for us—
yes, establish the work of our hands.
Lord, you have been our dwelling place throughout all generations.

Invite each person to turn to a person next to them and respond to the following questions:

- Where have you seen evidence of the Creator's care and presence in the generations of your family?

- Where do you long to see God's favor manifest in your family?

Chapter task check-in (35 minutes)

Do a check-in on the chapter tasks from session 1. If your group is larger than five people, divide into groups of three or four for this activity. Take turns responding to the following questions, allowing each person five minutes to share.

- What scripts from your family of origin are you repeating or reacting to?

- Where are you in the ongoing process of understanding and forgiving your parents their mistakes and limitations?

Hand out six sticky notes to each person. Invite everyone to write down three things from their family of origin that they hope to carry with them into their family and three things they would like to leave behind (one per note). Then divide into pairs and take turns sharing your responses, first what you want to leave behind and then what you want to carry with you (two to three minutes per person). As participants share what they want to leave behind, invite them to throw their notes into a trash basket. Invite participants to post in their book the sticky notes of what they want to carry with them.

Large-group activity (20 minutes)

Reconvene as a larger group. Invite each person to present the family purpose agreement they developed. After each person shares, cheer and applaud. Then pause for a moment to invite group members to affirm what resonated with them. After each person has had a chance to present their family purpose agreement, ask the group the following questions:

- How did you experience the process of developing your shared purpose agreement?
- What did you do to explore your family purpose agreement with your kids?

Announce and explain homework tasks (3 minutes)

- Read chapter 3.
- Identify your shared family rhythms.
- Reflect on tradeoffs.
- Engage in a whole family activity to explore shared rhythms. Try on a new family rhythm, set boundaries with screens or explore priorities with your teen.

Closing prayer (2 minutes)

Gather as a group and read the "Group Prayer for Family Thriving" together.

SESSION 3: A THRIVING FAMILY FINDS ITS RHYTHM

Session goals

- Celebrate the life-giving family rhythms practiced by group participants.
- Reflect on tradeoffs and any adjustments group members feel invited to make.
- Consider the level of intentionality required to live into a shared family purpose agreement.

Welcome and prayer (2 minutes)

Gather as a group and read the "Group Prayer for Family Thriving" together.

Chapter discussion (10 minutes)

Take a few moments to have an impromptu dance party. Put on some upbeat music, and invite group members to get their groove on. After one song, have a seat and discuss the following questions:

- What stood out to you as you read this chapter on family rhythms?

- How comfortable are you with the level of communication and the intentionality with time suggested in this chapter?

- What has been encouraging and challenging for you as you attempt to do a weekly family meeting?

Scripture (10 minutes)

Invite the group to consider how they feel about their time. Read the statements below, asking group members to raise their hand if they relate to the statement that has just been read.

- I feel hurried and tired.

- I don't have enough time.

- I should be getting more done than I am.

- I feel expectations and demands on my time from others.

- I fear that I'm wasting my time.

- I wonder whether I'm getting to what's really important.

- I feel peaceful and content with how I spend my time.

Have the group close their eyes and listen as you read the following slowly three times.

> *My heart is not proud, Lord,*
> *my eyes are not haughty;*
> *I do not concern myself with great matters*
> *or things too wonderful for me.*
> *But I have calmed and quieted myself,*
> *I am like a weaned child with its mother;*
> *like a weaned child I am content.*

Invite everyone to practice soul-quieting by sitting in silence together for five minutes.

Chapter task check-in (35 minutes)

Do a check-in on the tasks from chapter 3. If your group is larger than five people, divide into groups of three or four for this activity. First, have each person take three or four minutes to respond to the following questions about family rhythms:

- What are the rhythms that are most life giving to your family?

- What are some rhythms you would like to renew or a new rhythm you want to try?

- What whole family activity did you choose to do this week? How did it go?

Invite each person to spend three or four minutes reflecting on family-time tradeoffs using the following questions:

- What are the costs or tradeoffs of the decisions you've made as a family? Are you satisfied with the tradeoffs you're making?

- Are there any new decisions you feel inspired to make to have more time and energy for what matters most to you?

Large-group activity (20 minutes)

Reconvene as a larger group. Hang three large posterboards on the wall with one of the following statements written at the top of each one:

- Favorite family rhythms

- Best media-management strategy

- Lingering questions about family scheduling

Put on some music, and invite participants to jot responses on the posters, using markers provided. After everyone has had a chance to write something, step back and look at the posters together. Ask the group what they notice and are curious about. Invite several people to share more about what they wrote down. Before you move on, ask the group if anyone has a hot tip for living in rhythm as a family.

Announce and explain homework tasks (3 minutes)

- Read chapter 4.
- Reflect on your own spiritual journey and what you want to share with your kids about God's story.
- Choose a spiritual practice to try as a whole family activity.
- Talk about a new step you want to take to put your values and beliefs into practice.

Closing meditation (2 minutes)

Invite someone in the group to read Ecclesiastes 3:1-8.

SESSION 4: A THRIVING FAMILY DISCOVERS A COMMON STORY

Session goals

- Help participants feel empowered to explore the larger story with their families.
- Practice facilitating spiritual conversation and experiences.
- Affirm how participants want to live out their beliefs and values with their families.

Welcome and prayer (2 minutes)

Collect as a group, and read the "Group Prayer for Family Thriving" together.

Chapter discussion (10 minutes)

- What stood out to you as you read this chapter on discovering a common story?
- Do you find it easy or difficult to initiate spiritual conversations and experiences in your family? Explain.

- What's one thing you hope your family can affirm and embrace about the story of the real world?

Scripture (20 minutes)

Practice exploring the great themes of Scripture by acting out some stories together. Choose one of the stories below to perform together (or divide into multiple groups and have each group act out one of these stories). Take five minutes to read the story, and pick people to play various parts. Have one person narrate the story as the others act it out.

- The story of the prodigal son (Lk 15:11-32)
- Jesus calms the storm (Mk 4: 35-41)
- The feeding of the five thousand (Jn 6:1-15)

    After you've performed, sit down and discuss the following questions:

- What can we learn about God and ourselves through this story?
- Is there a new way you want to think or act inspired by this story?
- How did acting out the story help you engage it differently?

Chapter task check-in (35 minutes)

Do a check-in on the tasks from chapter 4. If your group is larger than three or four people, divide into groups of three or four for this activity. Take turns responding to the following questions, allowing each person three or four minutes to share.

- What have been the most significant moments and turning points in your experience and understanding of God and the larger story? Is there anything you wish had been explained differently when you were younger?
- What practice did you try this week with your family to help you experience God's presence and live into the larger story together?

    Invite each person to spend three minutes reflecting on this question:

- What new step would you like to take with your family to put your beliefs and values into practice?

Large-group activity (20 minutes)

Reconvene as a larger group. Invite the group into a show-and-tell about Scripture, story, prayer and presence practices. Take turns demonstrating a song, prayer or story-exploring technique you've found meaningful to practice in your family. If possible, don't just describe the activity; lead the group in doing it. Then discuss the following questions:

- What may be the long-term impact of having shared Scripture, prayer and presence activities as a family?

- What are your lingering questions and wonderings about pursuing a spiritual path together as a family?

Announce and explain homework tasks (3 minutes)

- Read chapter 5.

- Choose a whole family activity to try that fosters love and respect.

- Talk about your communication rules and practice resolving conflict.

- Reflect on where you feel vulnerable or how you're triggered by conflict.

Closing prayer (2 minutes)

Read the "Group Prayer for Family Thriving" once more together.

SESSION 5: A THRIVING FAMILY FOSTERS CONNECTION

Session goals

- Affirm the participants' desire and effort to create a culture of love and respect in their families.

- Build and reinforce skills for working through conflicts.

- Share and celebrate the ways families in your group build connections, have fun and offer hospitality to others.

Welcome and prayer (2 minutes)
Collect as a group and read the "Group Prayer for Family Thriving" together.

Chapter discussion (10 minutes)

- What stood out to you as you read this chapter on fostering connections?

- How do you relate to the complex role of being both a team coach and player in the life of your family?

- What's one thing you really like about how your family fosters a culture of love and respect?

Scripture (20 minutes)
Have someone read Romans 12:9-21 and then invite one another to offer short responses to the questions below.

> *Love must be sincere. Hate what is evil; cling to what is good. Be devoted to one another in love. Honor one another above yourselves. Never be lacking in zeal, but keep your spiritual fervor, serving the Lord. Be joyful in hope, patient in affliction, faithful in prayer. Share with the Lord's people who are in need. Practice hospitality.*
>
> *Bless those who persecute you; bless and do not curse. Rejoice with those who rejoice; mourn with those who mourn. Live in harmony with one another. Do not be proud, but be willing to associate with people of low position. Do not be conceited.*
>
> *Do not repay anyone evil for evil. Be careful to do what is right in the eyes of everyone. If it is possible, as far as it depends on you, live at peace with everyone. Do not take revenge, my dear friends, but leave room for God's wrath, for it is written: "It is mine to avenge; I will repay," says the Lord. On the contrary:*

"If your enemy is hungry, feed him;
if he is thirsty, give him something to drink.
In doing this, you will heap burning coals on his head."
Do not be overcome by evil, but overcome evil with good.

- Which instruction from this passage do you most resonate with?

- Which practice of loving relationship mentioned in this passage do you find most challenging or difficult to live out?

- What are the inner resources that allow someone to live out this radical way of love?

Chapter task check-in (35 minutes)

Do a check-in on the tasks from chapter 5. If your group is larger than three or four people, divide into groups of three or four for this activity. Take turns responding to the following questions, allowing each person three minutes to share.

- What kind of rules does your family have in place to support a culture of love and respect?

- What activity did you choose to do this week to foster connection?

Invite each person to spend three or four minutes reflecting on their skills for working through conflict.

- How familiar and comfortable are you with the conflict resolution skills that were presented in this chapter?

- In this chapter, you were invited to practice making repairs with your spouse or another family member. What did you learn from this experience?

- What aspect of resolving conflict do you find easiest? What is most challenging?

Large-group activity (20 minutes)

Invite each person in the group to think of a favorite activity that helps them have fun and feel connected as a family. Then, using posterboard or a whiteboard, take turns drawing out those ideas and have other group members try to guess the activity (similar to Pictionary). Play until everyone has had a chance to draw. Then discuss the following questions:

- How does your family offer hospitality and welcome to others?

- What's a new step you'd like to take to build deeper connections in your family?

Announce and explain homework tasks (3 minutes)

- Read chapter 6.

- Reflect on steps you can take to address your own personal growth edges.

- Have a family conversation about growth and change.

- Discuss your children's current developmental challenges and character growth edges, and brainstorm ways you can support their growth.

Closing blessing (2 minutes)

Invite someone to read Ephesians 3:14-21.

SESSION 6: A THRIVING FAMILY NURTURES GROWTH

Session goals

- Provide a compassionate and constructive space to talk about personal growth edges.

- Explore the connections between inner scripts and outward behavior.

- Encourage and affirm honesty about blessedness and brokenness in ourselves, in our children and in our world.

Welcome and prayer (2 minutes)

Gather as a group, and read the "Group Prayer for Family Thriving" together.

Chapter discussion (10 minutes)

- What stood out to you as you read this chapter on nurturing growth?
- What are the unique qualities and personality characteristics of the members of your family that you love to celebrate?
- What stages of development are evident in your household right now?

Scripture (20 minutes)

Distribute pens and paper, and have someone read aloud the passage from Psalm 139 below. Then invite people to spend ten minutes journaling using the prompts below.

You have searched me, LORD,
and you know me.
You know when I sit and when I rise;
you perceive my thoughts from afar.
You discern my going out and my lying down;
you are familiar with all my ways.
Before a word is on my tongue
you, Lord, know it completely.
You hem me in behind and before,
and you lay your hand upon me.
Such knowledge is too wonderful for me,
too lofty for me to attain.

Where can I go from your Spirit?
Where can I flee from your presence?
If I go up to the heavens, you are there;
if I make my bed in the depths, you are there.
If I rise on the wings of the dawn,
if I settle on the far side of the sea,
even there your hand will guide me,
your right hand will hold me fast.
If I say, "Surely the darkness will hide me

and the light become night around me,"
even the darkness will not be dark to you;
the night will shine like the day,
for darkness is as light to you.

For you created my inmost being;
you knit me together in my mother's womb.
I praise you because I am fearfully and wonderfully made;
your works are wonderful,
I know that full well.
My frame was not hidden from you
when I was made in the secret place,
when I was woven together in the depths of the earth.
Your eyes saw my unformed body;
all the days ordained for me were written in your book
before one of them came to be.
How precious to me are your thoughts, God!
How vast is the sum of them!
Were I to count them,
they would outnumber the grains of sand—
when I awake, I am still with you. . . .
Search me, God, and know my heart;
test me and know my anxious thoughts.
See if there is any offensive way in me,
and lead me in the way everlasting.

- How does God see you?

- What does the Creator desire for you to experience more of?

- What do you find challenging about holding the tension between your belovedness and brokenness?

Before moving on, take two minutes to turn to a person next to you to share what came up for you in your journal session (1 minute per person).

Chapter task check-in (35 minutes)

Do a check-in on the tasks from chapter 6. If your group is larger than three or four people, divide into groups of three or four for this activity. Take turns responding to the following questions, allowing each person three or four minutes to share.

- Where do you long to see growth and change in your life?
- What truth or true script do you need to affirm to be empowered to make a change?
- What practical action can you take to respond to the invitation to grow and change?

Invite everyone to spend three or four minutes reflecting on how they can support growth for other members of their family.

- Do you find it easy or difficult to have honest and constructive conversations about growth challenges in your family? Why?
- What do you feel are the important real-world conversations to have at this stage in the life of your family?

Large-group activity (20 minutes)

Chapter 6 suggested that parents can guide their kids toward growth and change by focusing more on internal character development than on external behavior or just following the rules. As a group, brainstorm a few typical child behaviors that parents feel challenged to address. Then talk together about strategies to address both the presenting behavior and the opportunity to develop character growth, using the questions below. Work through two or three scenarios. If your group is large, divide into groups of three to five people to work through this process. Try to talk about the scenarios generically rather than specifically in order to protect the privacy of participants' children.

- Name the presenting behavior.
- Name the negative impact this behavior has for the child and their relationships with others.

- Name the false scripts or unmet needs that may push a child toward this behavior.

- Name the good reality you can affirm that may help a child make a better choice from an internal motivation.

After you've worked through a couple of scenarios, gather as a group and respond to the following question:

- What's a good step you've been able to take to focus on character development with your child?

Announce and explain homework tasks (3 minutes)
- Read chapter 7.

- Do a whole family activity that helps you practice gratitude, affirm trust, express contentment and live generously.

- Reflect on what you want to teach your kids about handling money.

- Review or develop family financial goals and a spending plan, and start a conversation with your kids about money.

Closing blessing (2 minutes)
Have someone read the following passage aloud (Phil 3:20-21).

Now to [God] who is able to do immeasurably more than all we ask or imagine, according to [God's] power that is at work within us, to [God] be glory in the church and in Christ Jesus throughout all generations, for ever and ever! Amen.

SESSION 7: A THRIVING FAMILY CELEBRATES ABUNDANCE

Session goals
- Allow participants to name challenges to living a right-sized life as a family.

- Explore where participants feel invited to take new steps toward right-sized living.

- Share best practices in training kids to handle money and possessions.

Welcome and prayer (2 minutes)

Collect as a group and read the "Group Prayer for Family Thriving" together.

Chapter discussion (10 minutes)

- What stood out to you as you read this chapter on abundance?

- Where do you feel the challenge or invitation toward a right-sized life?

- Where have you seen abundance and divine provision in the life of your family?

Scripture (20 minutes)

Invite someone in the group to read aloud the following passage from Luke. Ask participants to listen to the text being read again and to pay attention to a word or phrase they resonate with. Read the text again and ask people to share the word or phrase that spoke to them.

Ask participants to listen to the text being read for a third time, paying attention to a surprising challenge Jesus presents. Read the text a third time and ask people to share what they felt most challenged by in the passage.

Then Jesus said to his disciples: "Therefore I tell you, do not worry about your life, what you will eat; or about your body, what you will wear. For life is more than food, and the body more than clothes. Consider the ravens: They do not sow or reap, they have no storeroom or barn; yet God feeds them. And how much more valuable you are than birds! Who of you by worrying can add a single hour to your life? Since you cannot do this very little thing, why do you worry about the rest?

"Consider how the wild flowers grow. They do not labor or spin. Yet I tell you, not even Solomon in all his splendor was dressed like one of these. If that is how God clothes the grass of the field, which

is here today, and tomorrow is thrown into the fire, how much more
will he clothe you—you of little faith! And do not set your heart on
what you will eat or drink; do not worry about it. For the pagan
world runs after all such things, and your Father knows that you
need them. But seek his kingdom, and these things will be given to
you as well.

"Do not be afraid, little flock, for your Father has been pleased
to give you the kingdom. Sell your possessions and give to the poor.
Provide purses for yourselves that will not wear out, a treasure
in heaven that will never fail, where no thief comes near and no
moth destroys. For where your treasure is, there your heart will
be also."

Before moving on, take two minutes to turn to a person next to you
and respond to the following questions:

- Did Jesus seem to believe in a world of scarcity or of abundance?
- Do you tend to see the world through a lens of scarcity
  or abundance?

Chapter task check-in (35 minutes)

Do a check-in on the tasks from chapter 7. If your group is larger than
three or four people, divide into groups of three or four for this activity.
Take turns responding to the following questions, allowing each
person three to four minutes to share.

- What activity did you try with your family to practice gratitude,
  affirm trust, express contentment or live generously? How did it go?
  What did you discover?

Invite each person to spend three or four minutes reflecting on their
family's financial goals and practices.

- Are you satisfied with the way your family makes financial goals
  and decisions? What's working and what's not? Share a new step
  you'd like to take.

Large-group activity (20 minutes)

Brainstorm a list of hot tips for teaching kids about handling money and managing material possessions, using the questions below as prompts. Document your list using a posterboard or whiteboard.

- What's a valuable lesson you learned in your family about handling money and material possessions? How was this communicated?

- What's a favorite technique for learning how to handle money and possessions that you've used with your kids?

- What's a step you've taken in your family to share or conserve resources so that all families on earth may thrive?

Announce and explain homework tasks (3 minutes)

- Read chapter 8 and the conclusion.

- Talk about the work that needs to get done in your family and how your children can learn and help.

- Reflect on the personality and passions of each person in your family and how you can support each other's development.

- Try out a whole family activity that helps your family compassionately engage the aches and opportunities of our world.

- Bring a meal or dessert item to share at the next session to celebrate the journey your group has taken together.

Closing blessing (2 minutes)

Invite each person to express thankfulness for one way God has provided for their family, using the phrase "I'm grateful . . ."

SESSION 8: A THRIVING FAMILY SUPPORTS PRODUCTIVITY

Session goals

- Reflect on family as a place where we learn to participate in the work of the world.

- Invite each participant to evaluate what they have gained from this process and discern next steps.

- Celebrate the journey you've been on together as a group.

Welcome and evaluation (2 minutes)

As participants arrive, have them complete the self-evaluation and feedback questionnaire below. You can make copies of this document to distribute to the group so that you can collect them and review feedback. If you've planned a celebratory meal, have participants fill out the self-evaluation and feedback form before they eat; you will get a much better response rate that way. This activity will help participants be prepared to reflect later in the session on their experience of the process.

Reflect on your experience.

- What was the most impactful aspect of participating in this group learning experience?

- What practices, tasks or activities were most helpful to you?

- What step have you taken in this process that you're most proud of?

- Which aspect of family thriving would you like to revisit and work on more?

Reflect on the group process.

- What advice or encouragement would you give to someone considering working through *Belonging and Becoming*? What do you wish you would have known before starting this process?

- What advice would you give to the facilitators about how this process could be improved?

- What are your ideas about what this group might do to stay connected and continue to encourage and support each other's efforts to thrive as families?

- Would you recommend this process to a friend? ___ Yes ___ No ___ Maybe

- Is this a process you would be interested in helping facilitate for others in the future? ___ Yes ___ No ___ Maybe

Chapter discussion

- What stood out to you as you read this chapter on work and productivity?

- What strategies have helped your family accomplish household tasks?

- What are some ways you've been able to teach skills and build capacity in your kids?

Scripture (10 minutes)

Have someone read Mathew 25:31-40, and then invite the group to respond to the question below.

"When the Son of Man comes in his glory, and all the angels with him, he will sit on his glorious throne. All the nations will be gathered before him, and he will separate the people one from another as a shepherd separates the sheep from the goats. He will put the sheep on his right and the goats on his left.

"Then the King will say to those on his right, 'Come, you who are blessed by my Father; take your inheritance, the kingdom prepared for you since the creation of the world. For I was hungry and you gave me something to eat, I was thirsty and you gave me something to drink, I was a stranger and you invited me in, I needed clothes and you clothed me, I was sick and you looked after me, I was in prison and you came to visit me.'

"Then the righteous will answer him, 'Lord, when did we see you hungry and feed you, or thirsty and give you something to drink? When did we see you a stranger and invite you in, or needing clothes

and clothe you? When did we see you sick or in prison and go to visit you?'

"*The King will reply, 'Truly I tell you, whatever you did for one of the least of these brothers and sisters of mine, you did for me.'*"

- Who are the "least of these" in your neighborhood and city—the most marginalized people facing great challenges and struggles?

- What are the great aches in our world that your family is most sensitive to and engages with?

Chapter task check-in (35 minutes)

Do a check-in on the tasks from chapter 8. If your group is larger than three or four people, divide into groups of three or four for this activity. Take turns responding to the following questions, allowing each person three to four minutes to share.

- What steps did your family take to compassionately engage the aches and opportunities of our world? What did you learn through this experience?

- Invite people to spend three to four minutes sharing their reflections on possible vocational trajectories for the people in their household.

- How do you imagine the gifts and personalities of your family members contributing to the greater good God desires for our world? What kind of work can you imagine them doing?

Large-group activity (20 minutes)

Take some time to reflect on the learning journey you've been on as a group, affirming and expressing appreciation for one another, using the questions below as a guide.

- What was the most impactful aspect of participating in this group learning experience?

- What practices, tasks or activities were most helpful to you—and what step have you taken that you are most proud of?

- What do you appreciate about the people you've gone through this process with—the facilitators and other participants?

Closing blessing (2 minutes)

Read the "Group Prayer for Family Thriving" once more together.

Shared Learning Contract

MAKING A PROMISE IS A powerful way to stay motivated and accountable while you're taking steps to grow and change. Consider signing this Shared Learning Contract as a group during your first session together:

I am committing myself to a process of developing skills and competencies to create a thriving family culture. I understand that this involves taking next steps with my family to become a space of belonging, where each person feels safe, loved, cherished and cared for, and a place of becoming, where we help one another discover and develop how we participate in the greater good. To effectively take my next steps toward family thriving I will

- participate in all group sessions,
- arrive on time to each meeting,
- contact the group leader(s) ahead of time if I have to be absent due to illness or a scheduling conflict,
- read the assigned chapter, and complete chapter tasks before the next session,
- share openly and honestly with the group,
- listen compassionately and keep what is shared in the group confidential,
- engage my spouse or a trusted friend or relative in this process.

Signature: _____ Date: _____

Group Prayer
for Family Thriving

Make our families places of belonging and becoming:
one in purpose,
together in rhythm,
united by a common story.
Help us connect with love and respect,
growing in wisdom,
living abundantly
and productively seeking the greater good,
so that our families and every family on earth can thrive.

Notes

CHAPTER 1: A THRIVING FAMILY LIVES FROM A VISION

13 *At one point his mother and brothers*: see Mark 3:21.

13 *Turn the hearts of parents to*: Malachi 4:6.

15 *Are you tired? Worn out?*: Matthew 11:28-30, *The Message*.

15 *Take [their children] by the hand*: Ephesians 6:4, *The Message*.

16 *Jesus knew this and often pushed*: "For whoever does the will of my Father in heaven is my brother and sister and mother" (Matthew 12:50).

CHAPTER 2: A THRIVING FAMILY CARRIES OUT ITS PURPOSE

38 *Individuals who grew up in families that were less functional*: Ronald M. Sabatelli and Suzanne Bartle-Haring, "Family-of-Origin Experiences and Adjustment in Married Couples," *Journal of Marriage and Family* 65:1 (February 2003), 159-169, http://onlinelibrary.wiley.com/doi/10.1111 /j.1741-3737.2003.00159.x/abstract;jsessionid=421211F14584A764B72ED 0FC205A6457.f01t01.

40 *Honor your father and mother*: Exodus 20:12.

40 *Learning to tell a cohesive story about your life*: Daniel L. Siegal and Mary Hartzell, *Parenting from the Inside Out* (New York: Tarcher, 2004), 31–52.

41 *Why have you forgotten me?*: Psalm 42:9-11.

41 *God sets the lonely in families*: Psalm 68:6.

42 *All things God works for the good*: Romans 8:28.

42 *Live in me. Make your home in me*: John 15:4, *The Message*.

42 *Lord, you have been our dwelling*: Psalm 90:1.

52 *Loving God and neighbor*: see Luke 10:27.

52 *Seeking God's kingdom*: see Matthew 6:33.

52 *Doing justice, loving mercy*: Micah 6:8.

56 *Hear, O Israel, the LORD our God*: Deuteronomy 6:4-5.

CHAPTER 3: A THRIVING FAMILY FINDS ITS RHYTHM

60 *When we repeat behaviors, neural pathways are strengthened*: Cathryn M. Delude, "Brain researchers explain why old habits die hard," MIT News, October 19, 2005, http://newsoffice.mit.edu/2005/habit.

61 *Not as unwise, but as wise*: Ephesians 5:15-16.

66 *Do not merely look out for [our]*: Philippians 2:4 NASB.

71 *In 1928, economist John Maynard Keynes predicted*: Elizabeth Kolbert, "No Time: How Did We Get So Busy?" *The New Yorker,* May 26, 2014, www.newyorker.com/magazine/2014/05/26/no-time.

72 *There is a time for everything*: Ecclesiastes 3:1.

73 *Count the cost*: Luke 14:28.

CHAPTER 4: A THRIVING FAMILY DISCOVERS A COMMON STORY

82 *Storytelling plays a vital role in shaping moral imagination*: Paul C. Vitz, "The use of stories in moral development. New psychological reasons for an old education method," *American Psychologist* 45:6 (June 1990), 709–720, www.ncbi.nlm.nih.gov/pubmed/2195928.

83 *Researchers often identify a shared religious core*: Leo Sandy, "Healthy/Productive/Effective/Optimal Families," http://jupiter.plymouth.edu/~lsandy/healthy_family.html.

83 *Are we human beings that have spiritual experiences*: Pierre Teilhard de Chardin, *The Phenomenon of Man* (New York: Harper Perennial, 1955).

84 *We live in a God-bathed world*: Dallas Willard, *The Divine Conspiracy* (New York: HarperSanFrancisco, 1998), 61.

85 *We see through a glass, darkly*: 1 Corinthians 13:12 KJV.

85 *We need to "create a proper container" of concrete beliefs:* Richard Rohr, *Falling Upward: Spirituality for the Two Halves of Life* (San Francisco: Jossey-Bass, 2011), 1.

86 *Jesus once described the mystery of life*: see Matthew 13:44.

86 *If you call out for insight*: Proverbs 2:3-5.

88 *It's a world that reveals God's invisible*: see Romans 1:20.

88 *It's a world where a loving, powerful*: see Psalm 145:13; Romans 8:28.

89 *Genesis describes humans as powerful*: see Genesis 1:27.

89 *Fearfully and wonderfully made*: Psalm 139:14.

89 *We live and move and have our being*: Acts 17:28.

89 *We know and love God by learning*: see John 15:9-11.

89 *We rule, for better or worse*: see Genesis 1:28.

90 *We're on a quest to learn how*: see Matthew 6:10, 33.

90 *The choices we make lead us*: see Deuteronomy 30:15-16.

90 *Which Scripture calls sin*: see Romans 3:23.

90 *We've become alienated from God*: see Colossians 1:21.

91 *Anger, jealousy, fear*: see Colossians 1:13.

91 *God is continually inviting us*: see Romans 2:4.

91 *Jesus Christ is the clearest revelation*: see Hebrews 1:3.

91 *As a gift to us, God makes the way*: see Ephesians 2:8-9.

91 *We learn to become all that we*: see Luke 14:27.

93 *God doesn't live in buildings*: see Acts 17:24.

94 *These commandments I give you*: Deuteronomy 6:6-7.

99 *Jesus once said, "Everyone who hears"*: Matthew 7:24.

99 *Jesus told a story about a feast*: see Luke 14:12-14.

99 *We take steps to live out the teachings of Jesus and the Scriptures together*: For more about this approach to learning and spiritual formation, see Mark's book, *Practicing the Way of Jesus: Life Together in the Kingdom of Love* (Downers Grove, IL: Intervarsity Press, 2011).

CHAPTER 5: A THRIVING FAMILY FOSTERS CONNECTION

106 *How very good and pleasant*: Psalm 133:1-2 NRSV.

107 *Do to others as you would*: Luke 6:31.

107 *Love the Lord God with all*: Luke 10:27.

108 *You shall not commit adultery*: Exodus 20:14.

108 *You shall not covet became*: Exodus 20:17.

110 *Rejoice with those who rejoice*: Romans 12:15.

110 *Live in harmony with one another*: Romans 12:16.

113 *Seek reconciliation with those*: see Matthew 5:23-24.

113 *When someone wrongs you*: see Matthew 18:15.

113 *Relentlessly forgive one another*: see Matthew 18:21-22.

113 *Making repairs in relationships actually strengthens the bonds of intimacy between two people:* Curt Thompson, MD, *Anatomy of the Soul: Surprising Connections Between Neuroscience and Spiritual Practices That Can*

Transform Your Life and Relationships (Carrollton, TX: Tyndale, 2010), 199.

116 *Research suggests that we remember negative comments and events far more clearly*: Alina Tugend, "Praise Is Fleeting, but Brickbats We Recall," *The New York Times*, March 23, 2012, www.nytimes.com/2012/03/24/your-money /why-people-remember-negative-events-more-than-positive-ones .html?pagewanted=all&_r=0.

119 *We need a source of love*: see John 15:1-17.

124 *Blessed are the peacemakers*: Matthew 5:9.

CHAPTER 6: A THRIVING FAMILY NURTURES GROWTH

130 *Continue to work out your salvation*: Philippians 2:12-13.

132 *I urge you . . . in view of God's*: Romans 12:1-2.

133 *Train yourself to be godly*: 1 Timothy 4:7.

134 *Do not let sin reign in your mortal*: Romans 6:12-13.

136 *Like plants in a garden, we are made*: see Luke 8:4-15.

139 *What's important is*: see Colossians 3:15.

144 *It's estimated that one in three girls*: The National Child Traumatic Stress Network, "Child Sexual Abuse Fact Sheet," April 2009, http://nctsn.org /nctsn_assets/pdfs/caring/ChildSexualAbuseFactSheet.pdf.

CHAPTER 7: A THRIVING FAMILY CELEBRATES ABUNDANCE

152 *The average size of a breakfast bagel*: US Department of Health and Human Services, We Can!: Ways to Enhance Children's Activity & Nutrition, "Parent Tips: Portion Size Matters," 2013, www.nhlbi.nih.gov /health/educational/wecan/downloads/tip-portion-size.pdf; and Margot Adler, "Behind the Ever-Expanding American Dream House," All Things Considered, July 4, 2006, www.npr.org/templates/story/story .php?storyId=5525283.

152 *The seed that fell among thorns*: Luke 8:14.

154 *A person's "life does not consist"*: Luke 12:15.

154 *"Do not worry, saying"*: Matthew 6:31, 33 NKJV.

154 *Jesus invited his followers to sell*: Luke 12:33.

154 *If we have food and clothing*: 1 Timothy 6:8.

154 *Whether well fed or hungry*: Philippians 4:12.

154 *Most essential to life is our connection*: see Romans 8:39.

156 *Can any one of you by worrying*: Matthew 6:27.

161 *Learning to be conscious and intentional*: see Matthew 6:10-11.

162 *If you currently don't have a spending plan:* For more help with finances and budgeting, see chap. 5 of our book *Free: Spending Your Time and Money on What Matters Most* (Downers Grove, IL: InterVarsity Press, 2013).

167 *One billion of our brothers and sisters live on less than a dollar a day*: United Nations, Resources for Speaker on Global Issues, "Hunger," 2010, www .un.org/en/globalissues/briefingpapers/food/vitalstats.shtml.

167 *The top 20 percent of income earners*: Anup Shah, "Consumption and Consumerism," Global Issues, January 5, 2014, www.globalissues.org /issue/235/consumption-and-consumerism.

167 *If every person used resources like the average American*: Global Footprint Network, "Footprint Basics," February 27, 2015, www.footprint network.org/en/index.php/GFN/page/footprint_basics_overview/.

168 *Average American consumes 195 pounds of meat each year*: United States Department of Agriculture, *Agriculture Fact Book,* chap. 2, "Profiling Food Consumption in America," 2000, 15, www.usda.gov/factbook /chapter2.pdf.

168 *Close to half the grain grown*: "Food Choices and the Planet," Earthsave, www.earthsave.org/environment.htm.

168 *18 percent of human-generated greenhouse gases*: Bryan Walsh, "The Triple Whopper Environmental Impact of Global Meat Production," *Time,* Dec. 16, 2103, http://science.time.com/2013/12/16/the-triple-whopper -environmental-impact-of-global-meat-production/.

CHAPTER 8: A THRIVING FAMILY
SUPPORTS PRODUCTIVITY

172 *God created human beings*: Genesis 1:27-28, *The Message.*

172 *We're learning to be good stewards*: see Ephesians 2:10.

172 *To be of use in the world*: For more about this approach to learning and spiritual formation, see Mark's book, *Practicing the Way of Jesus: Life Together in the Kingdom of Love* (Downers Grove, IL: Intervarsity Press, 2011).

181 *Only 50 percent of college students*: Susan Adams, "Half of College Grads Are Working Jobs That Don't Require a Degree," Forbes, May 28, 2013, www.forbes.com/sites/susanadams/2013/05/28/half-of-college-grads -are-working-jobs-that-dont-require-a-degree.

183 *Your deep gladness and the world's deep hunger*: Frederick Buechner, *Wishful Thinking: A Seeker's ABC* (New York: Harper One, 1993), 118-19.

188 *Yes, Papa, but aren't we called*: see Jeremiah 22:16.

GROUP LEARNING GUIDE

204 *Come to me, all you who are weary*: Matthew 11:28-30.

206 *Lord, you have been our dwelling place*: Psalm 90: 1-6; 12-17.

209 *My heart is not proud*: Psalm 131:1-2.

212 *The story of the prodigal son*: see Luke 15:11-32.

212 *Jesus calms the storm*: see Mark 4:35-41.

212 *The feeding of the five thousand*: see Matthew 14:13-21.

214 *Love must be sincere*: Romans 12:9-21.

217 *You have searched me, LORD*: Psalm 139:1-18, 23-24.

220 *Now to [God] who is able*: Ephesians 3:20-21.

221 *Then Jesus said to his disciples*: Luke 12:22-34.

225 *When the Son of Man comes*: Matthew 25:31-40.

About the Authors

MARK AND LISA SCANDRETTE are cofounders of ReImagine: A Center for Integral Christian Practice. They lead an annual series of retreats, workshops and projects designed to help participants apply spiritual wisdom to everyday life. They live in the Mission District of San Francisco and have three young adult children. Mark is the author of *Practicing the Way of Jesus* and together they coauthored *Free: Spending Your Time and Money on What Matters Most*.

Mark and Lisa Scandrette are available to lead workshops and retreats. For more information visit reimagine.org.

FREE VIDEO CHAT WITH THE AUTHORS

If you're working through *Belonging and Becoming* with a group of ten or more people, the authors would be happy to interact with your group via a free twenty-minute video chat. Simply be one of the first fifty groups to make your request by contacting info@reimagine.org.

Other InterVarsity Press Titles by Mark and Lisa Scandrette

FREE: SPENDING YOUR TIME AND MONEY ON WHAT MATTERS MOST

How you spend your time is how you spend your life. And how you spend your time is shaped by your financial choices. In the deepest sense, simplicity is an invitation to align time and money with what matters most. We were made to flourish and to do good in a world full of abundance. Yet so many of us feel crunched for time, stressed in our finances or perplexed about what makes life meaningful. There's a trusted path for recovering the life of meaning, freedom and compassion we were created for. This journey invites us to adopt soul practices like gratitude, trust, contentment and generosity, and practical skills like time management, goal setting and living by a spending plan. Learn to live more gratefully, creatively and sustainably. What's good for the soul is good for the pocketbook *and* good for the planet. (Group learning guide and session videos included.)

PRACTICING THE WAY OF JESUS: LIFE TOGETHER IN THE KINGDOM OF LOVE

How do we close the gap between how we want to live and how we actually live? So many of us want to live in the way of Jesus—pursuing a life that's deeply soulful, connected to our real needs and good news to our world. Yet too often our methods of spiritual formation are individualistic, information driven or disconnected from the details of everyday life. If Jesus of Nazareth demonstrated and taught a revolutionary way of love that's actually possible, alive with healing and hope, we need a path for experiencing that revolution in the details of our daily lives. This book explores how we can rediscover immediacy and action in our spiritual lives and offers a creative and active approach to spiritual formation that's intensely practical, combining the best contemporary thinking on kingdom spirituality with real-life stories of people who have taken risks to practice the way of Jesus together. (Group learning guide included.)